CHOOSE
AND
BRING UP
YOUR PUPPY

CHOOSE & BRING UP YOUR PUPPY

Kay White

With drawings by
Harold White

RIGHT WAY

CONTENTS

To the DUCKSCOTTAGE BOXERS. May they long continue to teach me the infinite benefit and pleasures of owning dogs.

1.

Do We Really Want a Puppy?

Buying a puppy is easy; puppies are very engaging things with all their desirable qualities on view. Buying the right puppy may be more difficult; dogs come in so many sizes, styles and shapes, and with such different abilities and temperaments that it may be puzzling to find one that attracts every member of the family. Not buying a puppy may be hardest of all, but it may be the right course for you, if you find you are unable to offer a good life to a dog.

When you take a pup into your home you take on a dependent relative for at least ten years of your life. You have acquired a creature whose needs, both physical and mental, will often be in conflict with your own inclinations; a permanent child given to behaving without regard to consequence, to living only for the moment. Your dog will have to be considered with regard to your plans for outings and holidays, his food and medical care included in your household budget, his crimes, mistakes and destructive rampages are your responsibility. Your garden will never be as neat again, nor your house as immaculate. Even the best-kept dog sheds hair, and brings in mud on his feet; he makes sniff marks on the windows, and grease marks on the doors. This is what taking an animal into your home will mean, and it would be wrong not to consider very deeply what you will give up for the sake of having a dog.

Freedom to be away from home on impulse is one thing you lose; immaculate furnishings is another. Owning a dog has, on the other hand, many advantages. The puppy will immediately add another dimension to your life, that of instant approachability by other human beings. Strangers will come and admire your dog, offer advice, whether you need it or not, tell you stories about their dog and recommend food, vets and training classes. You belong to an instant club which crosses all class barriers, and puts an end to loneliness. People will strike up a conversation with you anywhere when you have a dog on a lead, or a puppy in your arms. A dog with a bandage on his paw will make progress up the High Street nearly impossible.

Both at home and outside, the dog is your friend. We all need affection, and we need to be able to give affection, sometimes without the drawbacks of human involvement. The dog will accept our caresses with uncritical enthusiasm, and requires no complicated explanation if repulsed. Having few inhibitions itself, the dog does not mind when the veneer of social convention which we must show to the world is dropped. The dog adjusts to our mood, and while he may try to coax us out of depression by funny antics, he does not demand that his own ego is cosseted, and require that we listen to the story of his difficult day too.

The unstinting warmth of a dog's welcome, given without reproach for tardiness, is something that can be relied on and valued. For the only, or the lonely child, the dog can be a playmate, and a repository of secrets; a confidant who is always on the child's side. An over-disciplined child may also feel the need to pass on commands and slaps to some creature even lower in rank than himself. The dog may act as scapegoat for the child's misdeeds. The breed chosen must be carefully considered if this situation is likely to develop.

A dog in the family can also serve as a means of communication between people who have lost the way with each other. They may talk about, over, and round the dog. The introduction of a dog into any social situation breaks up tension; this is part of the value of the blind man's guide dog. In a practical way, the dog will guard your home; even a small dog is a burglar deterrent. People who suffer from agoraphobia forget their fears, and can even make successful exhibitors, when they sink their personality in that of the dog.

A well kept animal is beautiful. Grooming a long silky coat is soothing and satisfies creative talent. The shy and retiring person will gain in self-esteem if his dog excels at training classes. Dog showing is an all-absorbing hobby which will occupy all spare time and take you travelling all over the country, or just within twenty miles of home, as you wish. Every weekend, some weekdays and evenings you can be at a show. You may be asked to be on a Canine Society's committee, to help in the organisation, and eventually to steward and perhaps to judge. The dog fancy has its social side too, with annual dinners, lectures, teach-ins; even its own trips to American and European Shows. You can be a big fish in a small pond, and participate as much, or as little, as time and inclination will allow.

If you decide to own a gundog, you may consider field training, and spend winter Saturdays picking up for a shoot, being rewarded with lots of fresh air and a present from the bag; in retirement, your dog will keep you young and get you outside to the benefit of your health and spirits. Many a sufferer from coronary thrombosis has been ordered to walk, and finds a purpose and interest in doing so by means of owning a dog.

A new puppy in the house can be a frank child replacement, an object for care and consideration when the family has left the nest.

Dog breeding is fascinating, particularly if you can keep several generations and see familiar traits come through. It is not a hobby that will ever make a profit, and no-one should imagine that they can re-coup the original cost and upkeep of a bitch by selling the puppies which they may obtain from her. Dog breeding costs money rather than making any.

The dog you are considering buying will be a friend; one who never tires and never tells. In return, you must promise a permanent home, and the dog's greatest need, companionship. The dog can do so much for us, but we cannot turn him off and on at our convenience. No dog should be bought on the basis of being left alone several hours every day, if all the household are out at work. Some breeds will do a great deal of damage if they are frustrated and lonely. All dogs suffer deprivation when they are left alone, as they were (and to some extent still are) pack animals, intended to live as a group. Another animal may serve as some compensation, but the pet dog needs people, interest and activity, and so cannot be kept by a family which is away all day, even part of the time. A busy social life, or a hobby such as sailing which the dog cannot share, may also be reasons for denying yourself the ownership of a dog, for the sake of the pleasure you would get on the occasions when you would like his company. Dogs are not just for summer weekends; dogs are for day in, and day out, through some ten years of your life. A puppy will take time and patience to turn in to a civilised house-pet, and you will be lucky if some prized object is not ruined by his teeth during the formative time. Pups are not disposable, even when they go through a stage of difficult behaviour, when first enthusiasm palls, or when the family desires a change of life-style. Buying a puppy is the beginning of a permanent commitment.

When an old dog dies, some owners will say that they will never have another; they do not want their hearts broken again. Others will feel the only way to get over the sadness is to buy a new puppy next day. My own feeling lies between the two. It is difficult to laugh with a new puppy at once, so it is better to wait a few weeks, meanwhile giving consideration to the new pup which you will get. This way the new dog comes into an atmosphere ready to enjoy its antics without pangs of regret for the old favourite.

Owning a dog always costs money and the expense rises with the size. Initially you have the purchase price and the primary vaccinations. The cautious owner will take out an insurance policy with a specialist pet insurance company to cover the unexpected veterinary fees for those accidents and illnesses which we all hope will never happen, but they do, especially in a puppy's first year.

Rapid advancement in veterinary fees and techniques means that dogs can have practically all the treatments available to humans, including hip replacements and cardiac pacemakers, but the cost is high, and all animal treatment and medication carries Value Added Tax as well. A major operation, a long course of antibiotics, or extensive tests to find the cause of a skin problem can soon mount up to a bill of hundreds of pounds. But if you have comprehensive pet insurance, cover can go up to £2,000 for each illness or accident, you also have peace of mind, and you can tell the veterinary surgeon to go ahead and do everything to treat your pet, knowing that the cost to you will be only marginal.

Insurance proposals are available from most small animal veterinary surgeries. Insurance policies do not cover the cost of routine vaccinations and boosters, spaying or castration unless medically necessary, nor chronic conditions diagnosed before the policy is taken out. So it is as well to get your puppy insured as soon as it is eligible, usually at 8 weeks old.

The national animal charities can now only treat the animals of people who are on social security benefit, and proof of the receipt of this subsidy is usually required.

You should also budget for a wire-mesh indoor kennel, a beanbag bed, a nylon fur rug, and collars and leads.

Your other financial commitments may include boarding kennel costs, or a dog sitter from one of the many agencies when you cannot take care of your dog yourself. Terriers and Poodles will also need professional grooming services periodically.

Another important requirement for the dog is access to at least a small garden, or safe grass area very close to home. Dogs do not accommodate the use of a toilet tray, as a cat will. House training will be prolonged and difficult if you have to put on outdoor clothes and take the dog any distance before it can excrete in a sanitary way without being a nuisance to others. Control of excretory function is not really reliable until the pup is some six months old. If you have a garden, the dog may be quickly let out at any time. If you have to wait to get him on the lead and down the road, you are asking a great deal; it is comparable to taking a tiny child down to the public loo in the town every time he wants a potty. A tiny, carryable dog you might just manage; but if you tried to keep, say, an Irish Setter without any access to a garden, actual physical damage and illness could be caused to the dog.

Ideally, the dog must have a garden to which he can have free access in good weather. Secure fencing is necessary, according to the height to which the dog can jump. You will find that your dog deposits his excreta nearly always in the same spot, so you may check on his health and also easily pick up and dispose of the droppings via the sewerage system. If you have a sand pit for children, it is essential to keep this covered, as sand may be a favourite material for the dog, and more especially a cat to use.

Bitch urine burns grass, and there is as yet no remedy for yellow patches on the lawn though they are less noticeable on chalk soils. The adult male lifts his leg to urinate, from about twelve months of age. As well as bladder emptying, the stream of urine is used for marking out his territory, and objects in his ownership. You may find that some particular shrub or post is always used; the shrub will not flourish, and even metal posts have been known to disintegrate in time. If you have other dogs and bitches visiting your house, the resident pet will need to re-mark when they have left. This behaviour is inspired by primitive instinct, which it is not reasonable to try to eradicate. Ritual marking is a nuisance and leads owners to declare that the bitch is the cleaner pet.

If you are to have any peace of mind at all, your garden needs secure fencing, quite high if you are going to buy a dog of a large breed. A Boxer needs a 7 ft high fence, with an 18″ inward projection at the top in addition, if there is anything to attract him on the other side of the fence. On the other hand, he may be enclosed within 2½ ft of light wire, if all interest centres inside his garden. Heavy breeds do not leap so high, nor do small dogs, but they may dig under fencing, so wire and wood should always be buried several inches in the ground.

2.

Dogs and the Law

Within the last twenty years, in response to demand from the public, a number of new laws have been brought in which drastically affect dog ownership.

Possibly the most stringent and distressing is the **Dangerous Dogs Act 1991.** This Act, brought in after several fatal attacks by dogs upon children is more widely embracing than most people realise. Dangerous Dogs in this context means *any dog,* not just those breeds which are generally thought of as being biters. Even a Pekinese has been seized by the police as being a threat to a member of the public!

The Dangerous Dogs Act allows any person to complain to the police if they feel fear or apprehension about the behaviour of any dog, even if that dog is behind its own garden fence and is just barking at passers-by. In response to a complaint, the police will seize the dog and take it into custody. The owner will not know where the dog is held, and may not visit it. Eventually, possibly after many months' delay, the dog will be brought before magistrates, with expert witnesses on both sides, to assess its nature and behaviour. One of the most disputed aspects of the Dangerous Dogs Act is that the prescribed sentence is so drastic. Magistrates may order the dog to be returned to its owners, or they may order its destruction. There is no middle course under this Act.

Because the Dangerous Dogs Act has been used as a weapon in long-term disputes between neighbours, it behoves all dog owners to be very careful in the way they manage their dogs. Dogs must not appear to threaten anyone, must not even play in a boisterous way in a public park. As one veterinary surgeon has said "Dogs can risk a death sentence for just being dogs now!".

Another section of the Dangerous Dogs Act controls the keeping of American Pit Bull Terriers or dogs which appear to be of that type. Owners of this breed, primarily intended for fighting, have been obliged since 1991 to register their dogs and to have them identity marked by tattooing and also to have them marked with an electronic "chip" which responds to a special reading device. An estimated 10,000 Pit Bulls in Britain were ordered to be neutered, insured and kept on a lead and muzzled in public. These dogs may not be bought, sold, given away or bred from, and no more Pit Bulls may be legally imported. Among other fighting dog breeds banned from Britain are Japanese Tosas, Fila Braziliera, and the Dogo Argentino.

Most local authorities in Britain now employ dog wardens to advise irresponsible dog owners and to ensure local bye-laws are kept. Most authorities have brought in bye-laws which ban dogs from certain areas in parks, children's play areas and public games pitches as well as some beaches in summer. Many councils now require dog walkers to pick up excreta passed by their dogs and to dispose of it in a hygienic manner; some areas have special bins to receive it. These bye-laws have been made in response to complaints from the public who have become resentful that public footways and gutters as well as grass verges have been fouled by dogs to such an extent as to inconvenience passers-by. Fines for offenders can go up to £2,000.

Most owners carry a plastic bag or specially designed

"poop-scoop" in order to pick up their dog's faeces as neatly as possible. It is regarded as anti-social as well as being against the law to let your dog leave a mess where others may step in it.

Noise pollution by dogs barking to excess is also an offence which can carry heavy penalties and there are local bye-laws which make it an offence to allow a dog to stray persistently.

The 'dog licence' imposed on dog owners has now been rescinded.

3.

What Kind of Puppy?

There are so many types of dog, which will be the one to suit you? The first decision is between a mongrel, a typed dog, or a thoroughbred pedigreed dog.

The mongrel is a completely unknown quantity; bred, most likely by accident, from two dis-similar animals. The first cross dog, off-spring of two dogs of dis-similar breeds or of a pedigree dog and a mongrel, has no more to recommend it than a true mongrel puppy. Indeed, the first cross can be very difficult to live with, having its immediate parents' characteristics pulling in different ways, for instance a guard dog and gundog cross, which may produce a fierce dog which is restless and inclined to wander. Such dogs become a nuisance to own, or if suppressed, they may become neurotic through a split personality.

The mongrel is a gambler's dog. Very cheap to buy, but no cheaper to maintain properly than a pedigree dog. It will be unlikely that you can see or trace the sire of a mongrel puppy, so you have no idea of the size and the temperament which has produced your pup; you may deduce that he was uncontrolled and given to wandering. Because mongrel pups are seldom deliberately bred, it is unlikely that the dam will have received special care and feeding, or that the pups will have been reared with dedication and knowledge.

There is no truth in the often repeated saying that mongrels are hardier and more healthy; they are heir to all the ills that befall their pedigree cousins and are less likely to have had troubles attended. Mongrel litters are for the most part conceived by accident, perhaps by a bitch pursued by a pack of dogs, diseased, frightened and weary. Hereditary temperament and pre-natal infections play a big part in the health of the puppy and for this reason alone I would prefer a dog that had a better start in life, and was not born under a wandering star.

Three types of dog are not usually pedigreed but are bred to type for working purposes.

These are the Farm Collie, or Working Border Collie, which excels at Obedience and Agility Trials. These dogs have worked alongside man for many generations; they are quick and responsive, and their natural herding instinct adapts to the formalised pattern of send-away and recall exercises. If these dogs are not worked or given extensive exercise, they can become neurotic. Pedigree Border Collies have been recognised by the Kennel Club relatively recently and they now have beauty classes at many shows as well as being consistent winners in Obedience and Agility contests.

The Lurcher is smoothcoated and svelte; its make-up always containing some element of greyhound or whippet blood. Fast hunters and poachers, they are very much dogs to accompany people who work outside all day.

Jack Russell Terriers, and Hunt Terriers, and any of the other short-legged terriers that now go by the name of Jack Russell (although they are very different from those bred by the parson of that name) have quite a big following as game and lively pets and are cheap to buy, although they are usually deliberately bred and so have more care taken with them than does a mongrel. The colour is nearly always white with tan markings, the coat may be rough or smooth. The Parson Jack Russell Terrier, taller than a Hunt Terrier, has been recognised as a beauty show breed by the Kennel Club in recent years.

Foxhounds and Beagles, surplus to the requirements of working packs are never a good buy as a pet. They will escape at every opportunity and are difficult to house train as they come from generations of dogs that have lived in kennels and have had to compete for food. They will also suffer if made to live apart from canine companions. They have become institutionalised, and rarely adjust to a pet situation.

A pedigree should extend to three or four generations. The pedigreed dog may, or may not, be registered at the Kennel Club. If the pup is registered, or registration has been applied for, then you should in due course receive a computer print-out bearing its Kennel Club number and the names of its parents. This serves to authenticate at least the parents and grand-parents, although names at the back end of a pedigree have been known to be copied wrongly and to end up in the wrong places. If the breeder does not want to register the pup, the purchaser may do so, but the cost will be greater. If the previous generations have not been registered then it does get more difficult to register your pup, but if you mean to breed or to exhibit, then it is essential that the pup should be registered. For Obedience Competitions registration is not necessary for inter-club events, but for open competition the dog should be registered at the Kennel Club on the Obedience Register.

If you have in mind beauty competition or breeding, then you must take care that the breeder does not have the intention of getting the registration endorsed, 'Not to be bred from'. Such an endorsement is made if there is some hereditary trait in the line which should not be perpetuated, or if a bitch is too small to breed easily. An endorsement will not actually prevent you from having a litter of puppies, but the progeny will not be able to be registered, and so will lose value. British dog pedigrees are not identifiable as belonging to the particular puppy with which they are sold. Our whole pedigree system is founded on good faith and integrity, as there is no check on a litter by breed wardens, as happens in some European countries to ensure the right number of puppies is registered. Where there are several litters of similar pups on a dealer's premises at one time, identification can be difficult, and many people feel the time will come when dogs will have to carry permanent identity marking. Already it is possible to have a dog tattooed with its identity, inside the ear or inside the thigh. Veterinary surgeons advocate the insertion of a tiny unique microchip in the back of the dog's neck which can be read by a scanning device used by many local authorities and welfare organisations. The details of the microchip are held by the National Pet Register at Wood Green Animal Shelter. Your veterinary surgeon can advise on Identichipping. All dogs must wear a collar and name tag in public whether they are identity marked or not.

Serious dog breeders register and maintain their own prefix at the Kennel Club. All their dogs bear this word in their names, as in my dogs ... Duckscottage Pixie, mother of Duckscottage Dutch Doll, who was mother of Duckscottage Gorgeous, from whom we got Duckscottage Gorgeous Ruth. Ruth was sold to another breeder, having the prefix 'Balmoral'. Ruth's daughter, registered Balmoral Blossom, I bought back, and I added 'of Duckscottage' to her name, which indicates that I did not breed her, but I now own her. The breeder's prefix goes before the dog's name and the buyer can, if they wish, pay a fee to add their own prefix on the end as a suffix. No more than two names are allowed no matter how many times the dog changes hands in this country, but if one of the prefixes is registered abroad, then three are permissible. The Cavalier bitch, Millstone Duckscottage Jade of Loch Fee is an example of a dog which was owned by three different breeders, the Loch Fee prefix being registered in Ireland.

Champions are usually written in red on the pedigree. Other big winners who just missed being made a champion may have their best wins recorded under their names. While it is nice to have champion ancestors, points of beauty are not always passed on, and in buying a pet you will want to put more emphasis on good temperament and tractability. The pedigreed dog will have been bred, like to like, over many generations. You have the benefit of knowing what the size, coat texture, colour, and within certain limits what the temperament and intelligence will be. You also have an animal fashioned in a style which breed enthusiasts believe to be beautiful.

The Kennel Club lays down standards for each breed, and beauty show exhibitors try to get as near as they can to their view of the standard. Sometimes quite close relations are mated together in order to fix a characteristic. This is not in itself a bad thing, and does not necessarily lead to physical weakness or bad temper. If you find that a half brother and sister have been mated together, or that one animal appears several times on a pedigree, ask why. What was the breeder aiming at in doing this? There should be some definite pattern to the matings, not just convenience of having a dog to hand. Try to see some other stock that resulted from these matings, and see whether you think the breeder is doing the right thing. It may be that you have an instinctive stockman's eye and tell at once how a strain is working out. In many cases a pedigree that would seem closely inbred by human standards will produce a better pup than a pedigree packed with random unknown dogs of doubtful worth. A line bred pedigree − one with a strong influence of one prefix − will mean that you can get better information about hereditary illnesses, and if you are keen to breed yourself, you can make enquiries about the fertility of the bitches, as this is a strongly inherited trait.

The Kennel Club divides pedigree breeds into six groups: Hounds, Gundogs, Terriers, Utility, Working Dogs and Toys.

In describing the breeds and their suitability as pets it is inevitable that some generalisations will occur.

In a breed renowned for good temperament, it is possible to find a dog which is untrustworthy with certain categories of humans, with children or with other dogs. Bad temper may be caused by pain, nervousness, or some bad experience in puppy days from which the dog has not recovered. Early puppy life, from 3 to 10 weeks, is critical in forming character, and puppies must be treated considerately at this time. Bad temper which occurs later in life may be due again to pain and illness or to jealousy of people or other pets.

The top twenty breeds compiled from registrations at the Kennel Club shows only minor changes, year on year. Labradors are consistently Britain's most popular dog, for gundog work and also as tolerant, cheerful pets.

Labradors come in three colours: yellow (all shades from cream to strong red), black (favoured by those who want a dog for gunwork) and the rarer chocolate Labrador. Labradors were, as their name implies, created to work in cold conditions, so when kept in a warm house they tend to shed their coats copiously all year round.

Golden Retrievers come third in the popularity stakes, Cockers seventh and English Springers eighth, so giving these gundogs a very large stake in the hearts of dog owners.

Gundogs are energetic, docile, amenable to training and agreeable to other dogs. They are usually easy to feed, inclined to put on weight in middle age but always ready for a game with children. Other members of the gundog group are the liver-coloured Sussex Spaniel, the very elegant American Cocker Spaniel, the Setters, including the newly revived Red and White Setter (said to be the ancestor of the better known Red or Irish Setter), the black and tan Scottish Gordon Setter, and the very lovely English Setter, with a white coat flecked in blue, lemon or liver colour.

All Setters are tall dogs with strong tail action and they are "puppies" for a very long time. From sheer enthusiasm and joy of living they can easily sweep all the ormanents off a coffee table. It is important, therefore, to consider what alterations you will have to make in your style of living if you decide to take a large active dog into your home. On the other hand, kennelling one dog on its own almost amounts to a cruelty. The pet dog, whatever breed, should be a companion to humans in all their activities and not isolated from its adopted family.

Other Spaniels you may want to look at are the English and Welsh Springers, and the continental imports, the Brittany and the Large Munsterlander. The Italian Spinone is another import which is quite unique in appearance and has a delightful temperament. Irish Water Spaniels are curly coated all over and great fun dogs to own if you live near water where it is safe for them to swim.

The Pointer and the German Smooth- and Wire-Haired Pointers are larger dogs with boundless energy, more suited to working on moorlands than lounging around all day. The blue-haired Wiemaraner is one of the smooth-coated gundogs; a worker in a very smart suit.

Terriers have a distinctly different temperament. They were bred to hunt and kill rats and other vermin. Every sinew is alert, they are not easily put off from any purpose they have in mind, and their pointed muzzles are designed to snap sharply. They are therefore not the most suitable dogs to be around tiny children, but they are great companions for growing families. The many varieties of small terrier have some similarity, but when transport was a problem the regional variety of terrier tended to stay distinct. So we still have the drop-eared Norfolk, the erect-eared Norwich, the practical and unpretentious Border Terrier, the Lakeland and Welsh (both similar to small Airedales in colour and coat), the Cairns and the Scotties.

The fourth most popular dog in the pet-buying table is the tough, courageous West Highland White Terrier, a tireless playmate for children and adults alike and just the right size for a small house. All these small terriers are good watchdogs in the alerting sense and they are just the right dog for many owners, although if not controlled they can be noisy and over-excitable and so may give offence to others. The smooth-coated black and tan Manchester Terrier is always alert, keen and ready for action, and the Dandie Dinmont, always connected with the writer Sir Walter Scott, is a more unusual pet with a lot to like about him.

Many people remember the Fox Terrier, smooth- or rough-coated, as the dog owned by their grandparents. There are not so many around these days, but if you have a nostalgia for the breed, they can be interesting to own.

The Bull Terriers (the Standard and Miniature Bull Terriers and the Staffordshire Bull Terrier) bring a new dimension to walks in public places. They really do enjoy a short furious skirmish with most dogs they meet, and for this reason they must only go out with people who can control them. At home, and with humans, the bully-terriers are the sweetest dogs you could wish to meet and are usually reliable with children.

The Yorkshire Terrier is classed by the Kennel Club as a toy dog, but in the Yorkie's mind he is all terrier, alert, intelligent and capable of long walks as well as being dolled up with ribbon bows. His tiny size (up to 7 lbs in weight) makes the Yorkie an ideal pet for many people and he takes sixth place in the popularity stakes. Many owners of pet Yorkies have the coat clipped right down, for ease of grooming and so that the dog can lead an active life, but owners of show Yorkies must take care of, and intensively groom, the floor-trailing coats.

Hounds are the speed merchants of the canine world, bred to hunt and to run all day. Some hounds, such as the Beagle and Basset, hunt by scent, while the graceful Afghans, Salukis, Greyhounds and Borzios hunt by sight. Hounds do not figure at all in Britain's top twenty dogs, and it is easy to see why. Beautiful and graceful though the majority of large hounds may be, it is just too difficult to keep these independent, not very obedient, creatures in today's world. A great many are still kept, of course, but by enthusiasts who can devote a lot of time to them and those who probably have access to safe exercising ground.

Dachshunds, in two sizes (Standard, up to 20 lbs in weight, and Miniature, up to 10 lbs in weight) and three coat types (smooth, long-haired and wire-haired), have their admirers, as they are more obedient than other hounds, but they are still persistent hunters who will dig their way out of gardens unless the fencing is set in concrete. Dachs feel strongly that they should live in a pack, and they can also be unbearably noisy, as in former times, when used for badger hunting, they were trained to bark when they located their prey underground.

Bloodhounds are exceedingly large and powerful dogs, really only suitable for the specialist handler. Older Greyhounds, particularly those retired from racing, can be converted into lovely restful pets, and the same is true of the Whippet, a dog whose movement is a pleasure to watch and whose temperament is faultless. The Whippet is very fast over short distances only so he is more controllable than the larger hounds.

From the Toy Group comes a tiny hound version, the Italian Greyhound, weighing under 10 lbs, fine-boned and quick moving. This is a dog which likes its home comforts and hates to be cold.

From the Kennel Club's Working Group comes the world's most popular dog, and Britain's number two most popular dog, the German Shepherd Dog (popularly GSD), which used to be known as the Alsatian, and before that as the Wolf Dog. The GSD has done more for man than any other member of the canine race, being used by armies and police worldwide. The first Guide Dog for the blind was a GSD (many are still working in this capacity) and they are invaluable as Search and Rescue dogs in the mountains. Temperament is very important in the GSD; a bad specimen can be truly dangerous. When you start to look for a GSD pup consult local veterinary surgeons and dog training clubs, they will know where the reliable dogs are bred.

Collies and their smaller relatives, the Shetland Sheepdogs, have worked beside man on farms for a very long time. These breeds are intelligent, sensitive and easy to train, but they need a lot of exercise or constructive play, and they must be regularly groomed. Shelties can be insistent shrill barkers who may become neurotic if they do not get sufficient freedom. Rough Collies come in at twelve in the popularity list and Shelties at thirteen. The Bearded Collie, used in Scotland as a sheepherder, can be an ideal family dog, always eager to participate in what is going on.

The Old English Sheepdog enjoyed a popularity boom when it was featured in advertising, but many people who were attracted to this native British worker have found to their cost that this dog is beyond their means in terms of exercise time and grooming work needed. Some episodes of bad temper have been attributed to the fact that the OES wears his hair hanging over his eyes and so can be easily startled by an unwary approach.

The Welsh Corgis, both the self-coloured Pembroke variety which has royal favour and the more splashily white-marked Cardigan, are essentially cattle dogs, controlling the herd by nipping the heels of recalcitrant animals. These are active, intelligent, busy dogs, very well suited as pets to a mixed age family where country outings are often on the agenda.

Border collies have won many admirers because of exposure on television, but these willing and tireless workers need to be part of a man/dog partnership, both taking their share of an arduous task. This is a dog which positively needs to work and should not be kept as an idle pet.

A number of herding breeds have been imported in recent years, both from Europe and even further afield. The Polish Lowland Sheepdog is adaptable and easy to train, not unlike a Bearded Collie in appearance. Belgian Shepherd dogs (in four colour variations), the Portuguese Water dog, the Hovawart from Germany, Bouviers and Briards from France, and the dogs with the corded coats (the Pulis and Komondors from Hungary as well as the Nova Scotia Duck Tolling Retriever from Canada — which herd ducks) have all added to the richness of the British dog scene.

Another group of working dogs is made up of the guarding breeds which so many householders rely upon today. Apart from the GSD already mentioned, Boxers come out highest in the overall popularity list, at number nine. Boxers are not workers in any other sense; they were bred about a hundred years ago in Austria as guards and companions to man, and that is all they want to be. The trouble is they cannot visualise any happiness apart from their owner, so Boxers cannot be left home-alone, not if you want any home to go back to! They are ideal dogs, lots of fun to own for people who work from home or are able to take the dog about with them. The Bull Mastiff is much the same type of dog, but steadier by nature. Rottweilers, coming in at number seventeen in the top twenty, are wonderful dogs, gentle and loving by nature, but they can be dangerous if they are handled by the wrong type of person. A Rott. is not the dog for a novice pet owner, nor is the Doberman, another German dog which takes its guarding duties seriously.

The giant breeds, the Newfoundlands, Pyrenean Mountain Dogs, and St Bernards, are not always the genial nanny-type child minders that fiction makes them out to be. Too large for the average home, car and garden, these dogs are too much for the novice pet owner; weighing about as much as the average human, they require experienced control.

The Utility Group is the home for many breeds which do not fit tidily into the other groups, as well as the breeds which used to work but now have no job to do. Poodles, at one time circus and cabaret dogs, are a good example. They come in three sizes (Toy, Miniature and Standard) and are very intelligent and great fun to own, if you can afford the luxury of the six-weekly professional trimming they need. The Dalmatian, once used to trot behind smart carriages, is another out-of-work dog which longs for something to do. This is an excellent companion dog which needs a lot of exercise.

Bostons, French and English Bulldogs are part of the Utility Group. All these are smooth-coated and very well suited to a comfortable pet life, but they are all fairly difficult to breed and so will be expensive to buy. Japanese Akitas and Japanese Shiba Inu are among the newest breeds to come to Britain, as is the Japanese Spitz — a breed designed to be popular for its dazzling white coat which is not hard to keep clean. The Keeshond, once the dog kept to guard Dutch barges, is very attractive and easy to own if your house is not too warm. In their thick coats they do not need much artificial heat.

The Chinese Shih Tzu and Tibetan Lhasa Apsos and Tibetan Spaniels are the most popular of the Utility group. Small enough for the average home yet full of energy, and blessed with very attractive coats, they can be a joy to the family which can cope with the necessary grooming.

The Cavalier King Charles Spaniel is Britain's fifth most popular breed, as keen a hunter as any gundog, big enough for most people and yet not too big; cheerful, good tempered, and very attractive, they well deserve to be the most popular toy dog and are much loved by families who could not cope with a more demanding dog. Cavaliers come in four colours: red and white (Blenheim), black, white and tan (tricolour), plain ruby red, and black and tan. Most families want more than one Cavalier, and this is a good idea since Cavaliers live very happily together without any thoughts of jealousy or fighting. They deserve to be as popular as they are.

A newcomer to the top twenty, and a dog tipped for the top, is the Bichon Frise, a small white dog with a rounded face and dark eyes; very attractive and a devoted family member. The Miniature Pinscher, built like a small black and tan terrier, smooth-coated and similar in temperament, will fill the needs of those families who do not want the task of daily grooming.

The Chihuahua, from Mexico, is one of the smallest and most ancient of breeds, having both long- and smooth-coated varieties. Weighing only about 5 lbs this breed will suit those who have restricted space and exercise facilities. The Chi is surprisingly adept at keeping out of the way of people's feet.

There are many other breeds, some well established and some just beginning to be known, which are not mentioned here. It is not possible to "prescribe" a dog for any person or family; there must be some inbuilt attraction to begin with; and the dog must also suit the time you have to spare, and the place available for exercise, as well as the time you can devote to grooming. The inherent character of the dog is the most important consideration. You may get annoyed with the persistence and yappiness of a terrier, or you may admire their guts and determination. You may appreciate the detached and dignified bearing of an Afghan, or you may wish he was not quite so snobbish in his attitude towards your friends. You may rejoice in the boisterous goodwill of the Boxer, or find he is just about as restful as having demolition workers in the kitchen.

In the end, the right choice comes about by strong attraction between you and the dog which will be yours. You can make most breeds fit in with your lifestyle if you want to enough.

4.

A Dog or a Bitch?

Another question warranting family discussion is the sex of your pet; the right choice can make quite a difference to your enjoyment of the animal. The sexes are born roughly equal in numbers over the years, but it is not unknown for a litter to be of all dogs, or all bitches, and where there are several colours available, the dogs may be in the colour you did not want. Most people have very strong views on the sex they prefer as a pet, and it is as well to talk this matter out before you start to buy. As a generalisation, the male dog's attitude to life remains always the same once he has reached adult status, while the entire bitch is more prone to mood swings, excitable when coming into season, perhaps depressed and broody afterwards. It may be that the lady of the house who will spend most time with the pet, will have more sympathy with the bitch, which tends to centre its whole life round its owner. The dog is marginally less devoted, more outward looking and aware of other attractions. Among the smaller and more passive breeds, the difference in the sexes is less noticeable, but in the working and guard breeds of more forceful nature, the bitches are frequently significantly smaller in size and less aggressive in temperament. If you are attracted to a large breed, but doubtful of your ability to contain it, then a bitch may be an acceptable compromise.

There is usually no price differential between equal quality pups in each sex, though in some breeds the potential brood bitch may be more expensive.

The disadvantage of the bitch is that she has a season (heat or oestrus period) when she is ready for breeding. During this time she gives off a scent which attracts the male, and she also has a discharge from the vulva which will drop onto floors and stain furnishings.

The bitch first comes into season at between 8 to 12 months, and thereafter at intervals of between 6 and 10 months, varying with the individual. The season proper lasts an average of 21 days, but a dog living in the house would probably still be interested after this time, and may have been paying attention before the season proper started. There are now several preparations developed from the human contraceptive pill which will prevent the bitch from coming into oestrus or, less effectively, will arrest the period once it has started. It is advisable that you discuss the matter with your veterinary surgeon well ahead of the time the bitch is due. If you think you may want to breed from your bitch in the future it would be as well to make careful enquiries as to the duration of the contraceptive injection or other medication. Sometimes fertility does not return as quickly as owners had hoped.

The permanent way to prevent a bitch coming into season is to have her reproductive organs removed via the operation known as ovarohysterectomy, or more colloquially as spaying. This is major surgery requiring considerable skill, and although the operation is now performed frequently, it is not entirely risk free, in common with any other surgical procedure which requires a full anaesthetic and the removal of healthy organs from the body.

The cost of "spaying" reflects the care that is given and it is unwise to do as some owners tend to − shop around for the cheapest operation. It is preferable to discuss the whole procedure with your vet who has known the bitch for a long time.

Additional advantages of spaying are that there is far less incidence of mammary cancer in spayed bitches, especially when the operation is done early in life, and there is no risk at all of the possibly fatal inflammation of the uterus which can develop in aged bitches, known as pyometra.

On the down side, spayed bitches put on fat easily, so their food intake must be watched, and particularly in the spaniel breeds, spayed bitches tend to grow a very woolly-type coat over the hind quarters which defies grooming and spoils their looks. This is especially true in Cavaliers.

Sometimes spayed bitches will become incontinent of urine to a slight degree, especially in old age.

Although the ovarohysterectomy is the same operation as performed on women, bitches recover much more quickly. According to the recovery the bitch makes she may be allowed home in the evening after the operation, or she may require in-patient care for one or more nights. She will then need special supervision and restricted exercise on the lead for about ten days, until the wound sutures are removed.

Bitches can be spayed at any time, but preferably not when in season and not directly after whelping. Some veterinary surgeons believe in spaying bitches really young, at about six months old, while others prefer the bitch to have had one normal season and to have reached adult status in mind and body.

Preventing the male from breeding and all the behaviour patterns which go with it is a more simple matter as the surgery does not involve any invasion of the body. The testes are cut off externally and the wound heals very quickly.

A vasectomy is also a possibility, then the dog will perform all the usual mating behaviours but will be infertile.

Castration is sometimes used to cure aggressive behaviour in the male and is usually successful, especially if performed early, before the dog has developed the habit of aggressive or excitable behaviour. Castrated dogs are friendly, easy to get along with and a good guard for their homes, but their desire to fight other males, or to run off after bitches is curbed. If you are considering keeping a male of a large guarding breed, having him castrated makes him much more acceptable in society, and is no cruelty to the dog, as very few will ever have any role as a stud dog.

The castrated dog can safely be kept in the home with bitches, even unspayed bitches, and this may be the solution if you want the option to breed from your bitch but also want to keep a male. Both castrated dogs and spayed bitches may now be shown at Kennel Club shows.

It is almost impossible to keep an entire dog and bitch in the home, as the pair will find some way of getting to each other however careful you try to be. Even if you do succeed in keeping them in separate rooms when the bitch is in season they may howl, bark or cry constantly and the dog will urine-mark the territory in a manner which will not improve furnishings or garden planting.

The solution to the dog and bitch situation will have to be boarding one or the other elsewhere for about a month when the bitch is in season. And do not be deceived, the bitch will use just as much ingenuity in getting to the dog as he will to her.

You will recognise the signs of a bitch coming into breeding season easily. She may appear more excitable, and you will notice swelling at the vulva, and eventually a white or opaque discharge which gradually, over several days, becomes infused with blood. If you are counting the days of her season, the first day that red colouration is shown is Day One.

Bleeding normally continues for ten to fourteen days, and then gradually pales to opaque again at about twenty-one days after "colour" was first shown, although some bitches tend to be attractive to dogs for longer, and others will have shorter seasons or may show no colour at all, although they are capable of being mated.

It is best not to take a bitch in season out for exercise at all; she will come to no harm, and you will avoid bringing back a following of wandering dogs to your door when they pick up her scent. In fact, it can be considered anti-social to take an "interesting" bitch out on the streets. The preparations sold to divert the odour of the bitch do not deter a keen male. After the season is over, the bitch needs a bath to remove all odour, and possibly, according to breed, it may be advantageous to trim the hair from her hindquarters.

Some bitches which have definitely not been mated will go on to have a phantom pregnancy, showing all the signs of being in whelp, even producing milk in the teats and nurturing toys or other household articles as substitute puppies. Bitches which have intense phantom pregnancies can alter in temperament at that time and may be a danger to children if the bitch feels her imaginary puppies are being disturbed.

Some owners will feel almost obliged to let their bitch have a real litter next time but this is no solution to the problem; the bitch will have an even more intense phantom next time. The kindest thing is to have such a bitch spayed in the interval before the next season.

Entire bitches go on having seasons to the ends of their lives, there is no menopause for the canine race.

There is absolutely no truth at all in the legend that a litter will be good for a bitch, or that it is necessary to breed from her. A litter is a lot of work, a lot of trouble, and probably a lot of expense, which the pet owner does not *have* to incur. Many bitches lead long lives in excellent health without ever having puppies.

Prospective owners wonder what will be the right time to buy a puppy. Public holidays, especially Christmas, are not good. A new puppy needs treating like a new baby with a lot of rest, quiet acclimatisation, and should not be introduced in an atmosphere of noisy excitement. Many couples like to buy a puppy while the wife is pregnant with the first baby, and I have found that this works very well, both as an interest for the wife during the waiting time, and because the dog is partially trained before the baby is born, and almost adult by the time the baby is walking. It is not suitable to buy a puppy when there is a toddler of 1 to 2 years already in the family. A child of this age makes uncertain grabbing movements which are too rough for the pup, and the untrained puppy may be unhygienic for a child which spends much of its time on the floor. It is best to wait until the child is at least of nursery school age, so that the pup has peace and quiet for some part of the day; this is very important to promote good temperament, to ensure that the dog is not constantly disturbed when it needs to rest. Dogs already in the family are not normally jealous or resentful of a new baby, as people fear they may be. Indeed I have never known this to happen. When dogs are disposed of with the excuse that they are jealous I think it is more likely that the dog is now superfluous as a love object, or is making too much work for the young mother.

It can be difficult to arrange exercise for a big dog when the pram and the toddler have to be taken out as well. This is a situation which must be visualised and thought out before you commit yourself to a dog.

Nearly all dogs learn to travel well by car. It is best to persevere with all travel sickness and just go on taking the dog out with you − naturally on an empty stomach − until nervousness goes and the dog learns to enjoy the trip. I have found this to be more effective than giving drugs which sedate the dog, as every animal has a different tolerance rate for tranquillisers. Some dogs if given the recommended dose will be quite unconscious, while others go through a period of heightened excitement first. If you have small children and a large-ish dog, you may want to consider using an estate car with a separate compartment for the dog at the back. You may also buy a seat belt for the dog at a pet store; this is especially useful if you have a child in a car seat at the back and want to stop the dog from sprawling all over the child.

You must take the cost of boarding kennel fees into consideration when making your plans. Some kennels will not take certain breeds − those which pine or are otherwise difficult to keep happily. It is worthwhile making enquiries ahead of puppy purchase if you visualise using a boarding kennel frequently.

Boarding charges are made by the day, so if you are able to use a kennel close to your home you may be able to deposit the dog on the day of departure and collect him on your return, making a considerable saving.

Possibly the nicest time to get a puppy is in the spring, when you have the longer days ahead to enjoy its company, and house training is not such a chore. It is as well to be aware that most commercial boarding kennels will not take young puppies, they require too much specialised care, so if you have a holiday coming up, it is as well to enquire if the breeder will take the puppy back for the first holiday. Many people buy a puppy just after their summer holiday when they are settling in for the winter and social events are over for a while. One advantage here is that the glory of the garden is over for the year, so no matter if the puppy bounces on the flower borders a bit. Spring puppies who have got used to going in and out freely while doors are always open may have some relapse of house training with the advent of longer nights and the house being closed up; they now have to learn to indicate that they wish to go outside.

Puppies with Faults

There is a Kennel Club standard for every pedigree breed, a standard of excellence and conformation which, in theory, every dog of the breed should reach. But like human beings, individual dogs vary greatly and some will always be lovely to own but never be described as classically beautiful.

The standard of some breeds is very exact about placement of teeth and the correct bite. Gundogs in particular must have level mouths so that they will not crush game, and this criterion will apply even if they never go out with the gun. The Cavalier King Charles is a toy breed which must not be undershot for the show ring, that is, have lower teeth protruding over the upper ones, or badly crooked teeth. As these throwbacks happen quite often in show stock you may, if you only want a

pet, obtain a very nice animal because, as the breeder says...
'It has a bad mouth.'

This does not mean that the pup has any disease, or it will not be able to eat, but just that the teeth are out of alignment in a breed particular about this feature. Coats broken with white where a solid colour is desired, or plain brindles and reds when white markings are fashionable are other good buys, as the mismarked and plain dogs occur in every litter that also contains flashy puppies. Buyers often come to a kennel saying that 'they do not want a good one'. Of course, they *do* want a good puppy, one that will be healthy, strong and good-tempered. Anything else is no bargain at all. There are some defects which make puppies expensive even if they are given away, and you would be wise not to take such a pup even if you feel sorry for it. White puppies, especially the white Boxer, may be congenitally stone deaf. You can test such a pup at 6 weeks old. If he does not hear when a dish is clanged behind him, he is better off put down, he has absolutely no future. Puppies are sometimes born with only one eye; I have struggled with two of these but found that the disability made them nervous and wild, and at a disadvantage in exchanges with other dogs. I would now have them destroyed as soon as the condition became apparent. A puppy with an inguinal hernia, a lump in the groin, is not much of a bargain, as it will need an operation within months and may always be a liability.

A bitch with an umbilical hernia (a lump around the navel) is also a risk, particularly if you want to breed from her. It used to be said that the lump was caused by the bitch biting the umbilical cord too closely, but it is now generally accepted that this is a hereditary condition, as some breeds and strains never have umbilical hernias and some frequently do. It is just possible that when the bitch is mated a puppy might start to grow in the part of the uterus protruding into the hernia. Never take a puppy that cannot walk firmly on all four feet at six weeks. The tiniest puppy in a litter often attracts buyers, but a puppy *very* much smaller than its litter mates, even though it appears active, may have a heart defect which is inhibiting its growth. The defect will really make itself felt when the pup becomes adult, and may lead to disability and an early death. If you yearn for the tiny one, do get a veterinary surgeon's opinion first. On the other hand, size is unpredictable in some breeds, and growth quite often happens in fits and starts. A puppy that is somewhat retiring in the litter may start to thrive when it no longer has to compete for food, and may outstrip its fellows in size in the end. If you particularly wanted a small dog you may be disappointed. Even the breeder cannot give you a promise, but can only predict what is likely to happen through previous experience of the line. Some breeds, particularly those relatively new, or ones revived with the aid of outcross breeding, will throw puppies widely diverse in size in the same litter.

Male puppies should have two testicles descended into the scrotum by the time they are eight to twelve weeks old. A veterinary surgeon can give you an opinion as to whether two testicles are likely to appear. A not uncommon fault is that one testicle will be retained inside the abdomen. Even in a pet puppy this is a major fault which will affect the dog's health; not uncommonly, the retained testicle will become cancerous, so it is now the practice to have it surgically removed when the dog is a young adult. This surgery is not cheap, so it behoves the novice owner to think carefully before taking on such a puppy and perhaps to negotiate with the breeder about sharing the cost of the surgery.

With all livestock purchases, the saying "Let the Buyer Beware" is very apt and true.

5.

Where Do We Buy One?

Where are you going to buy your puppy? In every case, crossbred or pedigree dog, I suggest that you go to the place where the puppy was born, and that you do not buy from any type of middleman. See the situation into which the pups were born; see the dam.

It makes sense to buy as near to your home as possible, then you can make the best use of the breeder's advice. Ask the local veterinary surgeries, they know where the healthy puppies are to be found.

Crossbreds are frequently advertised in the local papers or sporting and equine papers. The best piece of advice is "do not be in a hurry, take your time, look around and be prepared to wait if necessary". It is worthwhile if you can get a puppy which is healthy and of good temperament and properly socialised to live in your home with your family.

If the pups do not look healthy, if the dam is a bag of bones with weak-looking eyes and a dirty coat, do not take a puppy. Feeling sympathy with the poor little thing is understandable but not practical, as you may spread disease to yourself, your children and to other people's dogs if you buy a sick puppy. If you are buying from a farm, ask if the dam has been inoculated against distemper, hardpad and leptospirosis. The last mentioned is a deadly disease, carried by rats which always abound on farm premises. Politely insist on seeing the inoculation certificate, and check that boosters against leptospirosis are given yearly to dogs in high risk places. This is too important to take someone's word for it lightly. If the certificate is not to hand, then you could check with the veterinary surgeon used by the farm. Canine Parvovirus is a disease of the severe vomiting and diarrhoea type which can be fatal in young puppies. There are now effective vaccines available.

Ticks, mites, fleas and lice are a nuisance which you do not want to get into your home via the new puppy. If the pups are kept on straw, if you see them scratching, or if you suspect fleas, take the pup straight to the vet who will supply you with an effective treatment of two types, one for your house and car and one for the puppy. That way you will avoid setting up a flea colony. I would advise buying the powder from a vet, as the wrong type could poison a puppy, which can take down quite a lot by licking its fur or its paws.

Take your crossbred puppy to a veterinary surgeon for a health check and possibly inoculation as soon as you buy it. If you know that the dam was not inoculated as may well be the case with farm dogs, then your puppy can receive very early protection which will be necessary for a little puppy going into an urban situation. The pedigreed dog will cost you quite a lot of money, so you must be even more careful that you do not buy on impulse. See several litters, preferably on separate days to avoid carrying infection. The keynote is, be prepared to wait, as at present the tendency among breeders is only to produce a litter when they have a file of orders which will almost take care of the number of puppies likely to be born.

The only sensible place to buy a pedigreed dog is from the person who bred it. BUY FROM A BREEDER is a slogan with real meaning. The term breeder needs some definition. Technically, anyone whose bitch has a litter is a 'breeder', but the producer of a first litter from a pet bitch, possibly by a friend's dog, is not going to be of much practical help or use to you. A great deal of knowledge goes into successful dog breeding; knowledge about the breed and the strains within the breed. The enthusiast gathers knowledge about type and confirmation, about breed habits and characteristics. There is also an awful lot to learn about the process of giving birth and the handling and care of the puppies for the optimum of bodily and mental health. If things are done wrongly, or not in the way recommended by the latest veterinary findings, then your puppy may not be the best possible value for money, or the one most likely to prove a good companion.

Unfortunately, many people think that there is nothing to know about dog breeding, that the bitch 'just has them', and they do not realise in what way they are failing. The canine race is basically very hardy, and most bitches are devoted mothers, so puppies of a kind are raised.

We are all apt to go into raptures over any sort of puppy. If you are buying for the first time, you may not be discerning and may not find out that you could have done so much better before your affections are committed to your new dog.

Because the skills of dog breeding are so little appreciated, you will find that the first litter type of breeder is asking just the same for puppies as those reared by people who have been a lifetime perfecting the art, so I say, avoid the 'pet' litter and go to a dedicated dog breeder, where you will find the dogs are not only pets, but a whole world of interest as well.

The 1973 Breeding of Dogs Act made it necessary for anyone owning more than two breeding bitches to obtain a licence to breed. Their premises, whether it is a semi-detached house, or a smart kennel building for a big quantity of dogs, must be inspected by the Environmental Health Officer to see that the dogs are well housed and well fed and kept in clean conditions with sufficient exercise. Fire precautions are also covered, and the number of dogs which are to be kept on the place stated. Once a licence is granted, the premises are open to inspection at any time, and a further big inspection takes place at the annual renewal of the licence. Here then is a partial seal of approval for you; buy from a licensed breeding kennel, and you know that the basic stock and conditions have met with approval by an independent authority. The Breeder's licence should be on view in a prominent place.

The fact that a licence has been obtained means that the breeder is aware of obligations and is trying to provide the best possible conditions for the dogs. To have several bitches of the same breed, particularly several generations of the same line, shows continuing interest and probably some expertise. Whether the kennel exhibits at shows is unimportant; a study of the breed at home from close contact with the dogs is the most valuable experience of all. You may, of course, prefer to go to a really big kennel housing several breeds and employing staff. Their puppies will be good too: they have a well-known reputation to keep up.

The very worst place to go is an establishment which just deals in puppies bought in from a variety of suppliers a short time before sale. You can identify such places by their advertisements for a multiplicity of breeds, and the fact that they cannot show you the sire or dam of any one of the "hundreds of puppies" which are said to be available for your choice. In the past ten years some areas of poor quality farming land have turned from sheep and cattle to puppy farming. These people turn out as many litters as possible from any breed which is in popular demand, obviously giving the dam and puppies as little as possible, as the only object is to make money, not breed interest or pride in achievement. The fact that they do not come in contact with the eventual buyer makes it fairly easy for them to get away with low quality stock.

These puppy farms evade the Breeding of Dogs Act, as they are in remote areas, unlikely to be inspected unless they voluntarily ask for registration as the more ethical breeders do. Puppies for sale are not advertised locally, but are bought by agents on behalf of the puppy supermarkets, located in the Home Counties or near big towns throughout Britain. The puppies are conveyed overnight in a crate, by rail or road, a journey of some two or three hundred miles with, perhaps, changes to be made and long waits on station platforms. Such a journey is very traumatic for a small puppy often under six weeks old. If infection is present in even one member of the consignment, it will almost certainly spread to all. The first frightening experience may be something the puppy may never completely forget; a lot of nervous dogs owe their bearing to this early journey, which the owners may never realise has been made. Although supermarket puppies are provided with a pedigree, there is no guarantee that it applies to the pup it is given with. An order for 10 black labradors may be made up by the agent from several different litters of approximately the same age — and who is to tell them apart? People who do not have enough pride and interest in their puppies to sell them individually should not be breeding and do not deserve your custom. You will also do yourself a disservice by not seeing anything of the background of the puppy you buy.

Prices at a puppy supermarket are no cheaper than from the owner/breeder, and after-care service is very much less. Often your receipt will bear the words, 'no responsibility taken once the puppy has left the premises'. There is one very definite reason why puppy supermarkets flourish and that is because they are impersonal. They have advertised opening times, formal premises, and if you fancy a puppy and have the money you can take it — no questions asked. If you buy from an owner/breeder, you first have to find one, then make an appointment to call, and possibly search for a house situated in a quiet area. Then you will inevitably feel that you are in someone's home; that the owner is always with you. You cannot make too many comments, whatever you feel, and you almost feel obliged to buy. You fear that you may be given the hard sell, that you are a captive client unless you make a break for the front door. Nothing will be further from the truth. You will find that a lot of questions are asked of you; you are put in the position of applying for a pup, and if you cannot satisfy the breeder, you may be refused if you do not have the right home for the dog. All this, and you are spending your good money!

It is with the best of intentions that we do not make puppy buying too easy. We do it because we care very much where our puppies go, and also because we do not want you to be dissatisfied and to find that you have done the wrong thing. Much is said about the number of puppies bought each year and then abandoned or sent to rescue homes. I do not believe that all those pups are lightly discarded. Sometimes there has been much heart searching, discussion, even threat of marriage break-up, before a wife can convince her husband that she just cannot manage with the dog; or a husband admits that he wants more social life or freedom at weekends than a dog will allow. Breeders try to save you all the agonizing and the sense of failure you will have and the general unhappiness of getting rid of a dog, by finding out if you really know what dog owning will mean.

Sometimes life changes radically for people, and they must part with a pet they love dearly, but in the main the unsuccessful dogs were unwisely bought in the first place. You may lie to the children when their pet is suddenly absent; you may even deceive yourself a little about this marvellous second home in the country, but you will know that you have done a basically cruel thing in passing on a sensitive and loving creature. You will feel especially bad if you know the dog has become wild and unwanted because you have never given it the company and the training that was needed. The owner/breeder tries to make sure you know what you are buying, and will also help and advise you throughout the dog's life if you have worries.

One of the best ways to get in touch with a breeder is through Pet Plan's Puppyline, an organisation which circulates a constantly updated list of puppies available from really ethical breeders who have to sign an undertaking that they will do the right thing by their customers. They are only allowed to sell puppies of which they own the sire or dam, so they cannot be dealers. Most breeders like to deal with clients who come through Puppyline, as they feel the buyer has gone to some trouble already to make a serious enquiry.

You may also obtain a list of breeders from the Kennel Club. There are also pedigree dogs advertised in the weekly papers Dog World and Our Dogs, and other monthly magazines devoted to canine matters.

It is wise to buy a puppy as near to your home as possible, all other things being equal. You may then take the puppy back to show the breeder at all stages of growth, and you may easily get advice when you need it. It never makes any sense to have a puppy sent to you, whether you have seen it earlier or not. The first journey from the place of its birth is a very big undertaking, and even the most confident puppy feels apprehensive.

It is best if the new owner collects the pup, or at least sends someone else to do so. Never have a puppy sent alone. First enquiries are best made by telephone, so that you can have a preliminary talk and make an appointment to see the breeder. Ideally, if you are planning really well ahead, you may visit the bitch before she is even mated, and put your name down for one of the litter. The bitch's pregnancy lasts for 9 weeks, and most really good breeders will have the pups all booked by the time they are 6 weeks old, so in choosing early you are working some 3 months ahead. It is not often you will find a really desirable puppy just ready to leave home on the day you make your enquiry. A friend and companion to last the family some ten years is well worth a time of happy anticipation.

If you have made contact with a breeder early, you will probably be telephoned when the litter is born to tell you that the sex and colour you wanted is available. You are not at this stage in any way committed to buy. First visits may be made just after the puppies are 3 weeks old. Before this time, the bitch needs calm, quiet and privacy, and will be acutely disturbed if strangers are allowed to see her and her puppies. Dog psychologists have found that the 21/28 day stage after birth is the time when pups are adjusting to contact with human beings. They should be handled and talked to from this time onwards. The pups will have started weaning, and the bitch will be feeling less acutely possessive towards her babies.

Who should go on this exciting first visit? I suggest you do not take the children for a start. Breeders do not like children to handle very young slippery puppies, as they are so easily dropped, and the children's high voices and sudden movements may be alarming to the bitch who is still a little preoccupied with maternal care. You also have a better chance, without children, to hold a serious conversation, and if you decide that you do not want to buy, then it is a lot easier to leave without the children wailing that you promised them a puppy.

In fact, if you are buying slowly and sensibly, it is much better not to mention the matter to really young children until you are nearer to taking the puppy home. Every older child, say, 12 and upwards, and every adult who is to be involved with the dog should be in on the purchase, and most especially the womenfolk who will inevitably have most to do with the puppy. Many breeders will refuse to sell to a man on his own, or to sell a puppy as a surprise present for wife or parents. It is much better not to take other friends and relatives just for the ride. Too many people present can be confusing for the breeder to talk to, and make an impossible crowd in a small room if you want other dogs brought in to show you. Friends get offended if they are asked to wait in the car, but really you are better to make the party as small as possible for this serious and important visit. The questions you want to ask, and the questions to be answered, demand concentration from both sides. It is unreasonable to suggest that the extra visitors should amuse themselves by 'looking at the other doggies'. The dedicated breeder is so often single-handed, and you will want her full attention.

Puppies at three weeks are still very undeveloped, but eyes should be open, ears turning down, and the puppies should be making an attempt to get to their feet with back legs sliding all over the place if they are reared on newspaper, as is the custom among breeders who keep their puppies in the house. The bitch will still be feeding them, and a pup will give a lusty yell if he loses his teat. The pups should look clean with glistening fur, and smell nice. Damp, dirty puppies making a thin wailing cry, mean disease. Go out of the door quickly, and do not go to another kennel the same day. The dam will be still cleaning up the excreta of her puppies as it is passed, although if they have started weaning and are taking solid food she may begin to stop doing so.

The bitch may growl a little when you approach. This is perfectly normal; she should be a little apprehensive for her babies, and warn you not to take liberties. You will have had opportunity to assess her temperament in normal circumstances, either before she whelped or later when her pups are independent.

One copy of the pedigree should be available for you to see at this viewing. About now the breeder will be sending up a registration form to the Kennel Club if the puppies are to be registered. There is often some delay in the return of the cards due to pressure of work at the Kennel Club, so it is customary to get the registrations off as soon as names have been decided, and it is evident that all the puppies are going to thrive. The colours and textures of the coats may not be the same as the adult; this is true in many breeds. Markings can be deceptive at this stage. When the puppies are lying flat they will appear to have more white than will be apparent when they are on their feet. It is also possible that when the coat is more profuse, isolated markings may run together, or small white flashes may be obscured. If white markings are important to you, too much white is better at this stage than barely enough.

Since 1992 it has been illegal for anyone other than a qualified veterinary surgeon to shorten (dock) a puppy's tail. At the same time, the Royal College of Veterinary Surgeons (the vet's governing body) advised their members that tail docking to conform with a conventional standard is an unjustified

mutilation and unethical, unless docking is necessary to treat
a tail injury or as a means of preventing injury which is in the
interest of the dog in view of its predicted lifestyle, i.e. in
gundogs working in cover.

Accordingly, the majority of veterinary surgeons have
ceased to provide a docking service for puppies, although
some will use their own discretion on docking, usually
docking puppy tails only for their own breeder clients,
although a vet who docks tails without due reason runs the risk
of disciplinary action being taken against him by the RCVS.

Dew claws, the extra claw at 'ankle' level, may still be
removed in the majority of breeds because of the risk of the
claw being torn off. Both docking and dew claw removal
are carried out on puppies soon after birth, at two or three
days old.

It is therefore important, if you are buying a puppy in a
breed which is customarily docked, that you make the fullest
enquiries of the breeder well before the litter is born.

The Kennel Club Breed Standards now allow for all
breeds, including those where dogs have been customarily
docked, to be exhibited with or without full tails and show
judges are instructed to give docked and undocked
specimens equal consideration.

When examining four week old puppies, see that the navel
is clean and free from inflammation. The first baby teeth
should be through the gums. Nails should be clipped neatly
and not hooked.

6.

Choosing a Puppy

It is too early to put a deposit on the purchase of a puppy at three weeks of age unless you are very confident of the breeder and quite sure of what you want. You can say at this stage that you are very interested, and make another appointment to return. The price now stated for the puppies will differ between show specimens and companion animals, but it is really too early to decide on the potential of any puppy, no matter what claims the breeder may make.

You could ask at this time for the address where the sire is kept and make an appointment to see him too. The owner of the sire should not object as he or she will be helping to see that the pups are well sold. The decisive visit to the puppies will be made at 4½ to 5 weeks. All the pups should be walking now and eating solid food, although they will run to the dam when she visits them. You can tell a lot by the quality of the excreta in the puppy pen, it should be firm and formed, not loose and runny. The colour varies according to the feed they last had; a milk or a meat one. Liquid excreta deposited in an explosive way while you are watching indicates a digestive upset. This will not be a reason for rejecting a puppy at this stage if all else pleases, but I would want to see a better performance next time. If the puppies are being wormed that day, then messy excreta can be excused.

You should be able to handle the puppies more freely on this visit, and be allowed to let them run outside the playpen. The pups may look a little more messy this time, as when they are beginning to eat solid food they frequently get it all over themselves. In a litter that is very much of one colour, any puppies that are chosen should be removed and kept separately, as it is often difficult to identify the puppy that a family took so long in choosing. The bitch may be resting somewhere apart or running about freely. She should not be shut up with her growing pups so that they can torment her. This is a sign of bad and unkind management and will not be a recommendation to you. The bitch may be losing her coat; many breeds do after whelping. Her teats may be well pulled down and she will perhaps look thin, but she should be happy, groomed and well cared for.

The pups should be warm enough or shaded from the sun, according to the season. They should be in clean surroundings and in close contact with human beings. It will be important to you that the pups have heard household noises and been talked to and otherwise thoroughly accustomed to life among people. Pups reared a long way from the house in a kennel are never as friendly later on as those which are humanized early. Pups at about 5 weeks sleep a lot, but play furiously together in short bouts.

It would be misleading to label one as the quiet one and one the out-going one, as that individual may be just more sleepy, or more energetic at this time; or perhaps he ate more at the last meal. Even if all the pups are sleepy and lethargic, it may only mean that you caught them at their afternoon nap. Provided they look healthy, they are better doing what comes naturally. "Lovely fat puppies" is the greatest mis-nomer on earth. Puppies should not be carrying fat which will put too much strain on developing leg and shoulder joints. Pups should be lean and heavy for their size in all breeds. A large fat belly is not so much likely to be full of food as full of roundworms.

Eyes should be bright and there should be no purulent discharge from eyes or nose. Pups may be play-barking, or play fighting; they should not be wailing miserably. Just at this age they are trying their skills; the amount of barking you hear now is not typical of the animal when it is older. If you watch the pups at play you may see that one is always the aggressor, challenging the others, stirring things up. That one is likely to be a strong character, and if you are buying in a large and forceful breed, this pup may be more than you wish to take on. Another strong willed fellow will be climbing up the corner of the play pen determined to get where he wants. He may be fun, but also hard work.

The pup sitting watching, working things out, may in the end be the most clever and most trainable. Even at this age you will discover the pup that is cuddly, and the one that squirms away, anxious to get down and be exploring. If you are buying a pup purely as a pet it is better to buy for character indications than for colour markings.

If you want a puppy reserved for you, you must now offer a deposit of one third of the purchase price. If you fail to collect the puppy and complete the purchase, the breeder is entitled to keep the deposit. It is understandable that there is an optimum time for selling puppies, and if a pup is kept for you and you fail to complete the bargain, then the breeder has been put to trouble and expense and missed other opportunities. When you have put down a deposit you should receive a receipt, quoting by name or description exactly which puppy it concerns, and also a feeding chart and some details about the regime the puppy is used to. Most good kennels give quite a lot of detail about the breed, with information about the books to buy and breed clubs. You should be told what food to get ready for the puppy's arrival, and also what simple home first-aid items to buy. Some breeders will give the puppy packed meals for one day, so that you may see exactly the size and consistency the puppy has been used to.

Even if eventually you mean to feed the puppy in a different way, it is important to continue for at least two weeks with the routine used by the breeder, and to feed exactly the same foods, but increasing the quantity if the puppy can take it towards the end of the fortnight. Leaving its first home is quite enough upset for a puppy without altering the diet too. It is important to use the same foods right down to the quality of milk given. Using a richer milk is quite sufficient to bring on a looseness of the bowels.

Many people feel that it would be a sensible safeguard to have a veterinary surgeon examine the puppy of their choice before they finally seal the bargain. Some books will advise you to ask the breeder if you may take the puppy to a vet. As a breeder, I am totally unwilling that you should take a puppy away to a veterinary surgery where it may run the risk of being infected, and then expect me to take it back if you reject it. In the meantime you will have subjected the puppy to many new experiences; you may have handled it badly and passed it all round the neighbours for all I know. For the protection of other buyers, no puppy which has left my premises can come back until well after the first inoculation dose. It certainly does make sense to have a veterinary examination, but you must ask a vet to visit my kennels.

If you live at a distance it will be expensive to ask your local veterinary surgeon to make a journey to a kennel, so you will have to use a practice local to me. Such is the integrity of the veterinary profession, a certificate of good health will not be given to a suspect puppy, even if the breeder happens to be the vet's own client.

What Age to Buy

The question now arises, at what age should you take your puppy to its new home? The answer rather depends on the breed, the amount of time you have to give to the puppy's care, the inmates of your household, and your fondness for caring for the very young. In a big breed, strong puppies are able to go at 6 weeks old, to a family of adults who will allow the puppy a lot of rest and are willing to give a lot of care. A puppy as young as this is very dependent, but becomes completely imprinted with its new owners. A 6 week old puppy cannot ever be expected to spend the nights in a kitchen alone, so you must leave the collection until later if you are very much against animals in the bedroom, unless you are willing to camp in the kitchen with the pup. Puppies of a very small breed will be too fragile to leave as young as this. At one time 8 weeks was the standard time for taking puppies, but lately dog psychologists have found that 8 weeks of age in a puppy equates with the 8 month 'fear' period in a human baby, so it is better if no disturbing experiences occur at this time. So if you do not take your puppy at 6-7 weeks, it may be best to leave it with the breeder until 9-10 weeks, but only if the pup is kept in the house and the breeder takes trouble to socialise the puppy by allowing it to meet a variety of people and hear all the household noises.

I like my new owners to collect their puppies at mid-morning: most of them do so on a Saturday in order to have the whole weekend with the puppy. Two people should come to collect so that one may hold the puppy securely in their arms, wrapped in a blanket if it is winter, while the other drives. I do not like puppies put in a box in the back of a car; they need the reassurance of a human so that the first journey will be as happy as possible. A towel and some tissues are useful things to have in the car, in case the puppy drools or is sick. It will not be likely to urinate until put to the ground, which should not be until you are in your own garden.

Many breeders now include in the puppy's purchase price short-term insurance cover for the first six weeks in the new home. The cost is very small, whether the purchaser pays for it or the breeder includes it as a gift. Make sure that the insurance on your puppy comes into operation immediately the pup leaves the breeder's premises, including cover for the journey to the new home.

This short-term cover for the puppy should include veterinary fees for accident and illness and refund of purchase price if the worst happens and the pup should die.

Puppies are extremely vulnerable when they change homes, both to infections and poisonings as well as accidents through their own desire to explore their surroundings, so this puppy cover protects the breeder as well as the new owner in that the breeder will not have to consider the financial loss involved in giving the purchase price back if there is any dispute about illness or death.

Before the six weeks' puppy cover expires the insurance company should contact you about taking out permanent insurance for the puppy and this is well worth doing because puppies are risk-laden and completely unpredictable.

What to Expect from the Breeder

1. The pedigree of the puppy, correctly made out and signed.
2. Receipt for purchase price, less deposit if one was made.
3. Feeding chart and helpful information.
4. Registration card and signed transfer form (if back from Kennel Club), or signed form for you to register puppy yourself.
5. Advice as necessary for at least a few weeks after puppy is taken.
6. A healthy, sound puppy, free of fleas and lice, wormed twice, accustomed to handling, and able to eat enough solid and liquid food for its complete maintenance.
7. A puppy fit for the purpose you have made clear at the time of purchase.
8. That you may unquestioningly receive your money back (not the offer of another puppy) if the puppy is not up to the standard of health required within the first 7 days after purchase. Naturally, a veterinary certificate will be needed if you are complaining of a sub-standard puppy.

What the Vendor Will Expect From You

1. That you will have told the truth about the purpose for which you require the puppy, and about the life it will lead.
2. That the puppy is intended for the people presenting

themselves as buyers, and that it is not for re-sale for any purpose whatever.

3. That you have made adequate provision for the puppy at home, fenced the garden securely and provided a warm place to sleep.

4. That you have already made contact with a private veterinary surgeon for the puppy's preventative inoculations, and for any treatment needed in the future.

5. That you come to collect the puppy provided with the balance of money due, either in cash or a cheque supported by a bankers card.

Puppies are not sold on easy terms. To ask for such a concession proves at once that you are seeking 'instant gratification' for something you cannot afford. This may work all right with household appliances but not with a creature that eats. No ethical breeder will sell on easy terms, nor will they sell puppies on approval — no-one who understands or cares about dogs could countenance this method.

You cannot expect the breeder to give you a lifetime guarantee of good health for the puppy. In a living animal many things occur which are not apparent in babyhood. Provided that the breeder has taken all possible steps to breed a healthy puppy and hands it to you in that condition, you really have not any cause for complaint, whatever happens afterwards. Even a veterinary surgeon can only tell you that the puppy appears absolutely normal at the time he examines it.

You cannot expect that a puppy will be house trained before it is six months old. If you call infantile lack of bladder or bowel control in humans or dogs 'dirty', then a puppy is a dirty thing to have in your home. Don't buy one. Some puppies house train more quickly than others, but some accidents and lapse of control during long nights should be expected right up to the age of nine months, and again in sick or very old dogs.

Comparison of Development of Child & Puppy

	Child	Puppy
Hearing present	at birth	3 weeks
Sight (both prefer dim light)	at birth	1-2 weeks
Adult sight	2 years	8 weeks
Stand	9 months	3 weeks
Walk	12 months	4 weeks
Teething (primary)	up to 3 years	2 weeks
Permanent teeth	6 years	4 months
Recognise & respond to people	3 months	4 weeks
No urination during sleep	4 years	4 weeks
Able to indicate need to urinate & wait a few minutes	18 months	10 weeks
Urination mainly controlled	4 years	7 months
Play sensibly with own age group	10 months	5 weeks
Understand and carry out requests	18 months	3-4 months
Understand "No!"	1 year	4 months

You cannot expect any absolute declaration that a puppy will make a good brood bitch, guard or show specimen. Nothing more definite is possible than 'it is likely to'. Beware of people who advertise a litter of 'Champion' puppies. The term Champion has a specific meaning in show dog language, and there is a risk of running foul of the Trades Description Act if this word is used to describe anything other than an animal which has been exhibited and won its way to Champion status.

Puppies may correctly be described as 'puppies from Champion parents, or stock', but not Champion puppies.

If the puppy which you bought should develop a disease in later life which could be described as being hereditary, it is a kindness to inform the breeder, without reproach or blame, but as a piece of knowledge which may help in future breeding plans. I hope that the news will be received by the breeder with regret and courtesy.

You can never expect to recoup the purchase price of the puppy if you have to part with it for reasons of your own. Once the normal selling time is passed, the value of a pup drops rapidly. Very few people want older puppies or grown dogs; they want the pleasure of a little puppy, as you did. If something so drastic happens that you are forced to part with your new puppy within a few weeks, the best the breeder can do for you is to board the pup and sell it at the best possible price to a permanent home. This is a kindness and a concession to you, and you should not be demanding about it, or hope for very much money back. New advertisements may have to be placed and time taken to interview other owners, who will want to know why the puppy was returned and may be dubious about buying at full price. In livestock particularly, a bad buy is almost always a total loss − another reason for not buying on impulse.

Aside from failing a health check in early days, the breeder is not obliged to take back your dog, for whatever reason you have to part with it. If you have kept in touch in a friendly manner, you can certainly talk over the problem and see if the breeder can advise you. Now that most breeders are limited in the numbers they can kennel by the Breeding of Dogs Act, it is increasingly impossible to receive grown animals back to the premises.

It is likely that if the dog must go, you will have to advertise, interview, and dispose of the dog yourself. This is not a very pleasant thing to have to do, so it is all the more important to regard the puppy you buy as a permanent member of the family, which you cannot part from any more than you would a child. If the breeder's questions at the first interview reveal that you have a different attitude, and you are told that you are not in the position to give the dog the right home, try to be grateful for the breeder's honesty, for you will have been spared considerable expense and unhappiness.

7.

Getting Ready for a Puppy

All dogs should be inoculated against five potentially fatal diseases: Distemper, Canine Virus Hepatitis, Canine Parvovirus and two varieties of Leptospirosis. Your puppy will probably not have begun the course of vaccinations when you collect it, but you should be assured that the dam and other dogs on the breeder's premises are vaccinated and given annual or bi-annual booster vaccinations as the vet advises.

The vaccination course has become quite complicated and it is as well to have discussed the programme for your puppy with the vet of your choice. If you are buying from a local kennel your vet may advise you to take special precautions in view of any local epidemics or the weight of infection likely to prevail in the kennel in question.

There has, in some quarters, been a fashion for using homeopathic vaccines, avoiding any consultation with the vet. Since these vaccines are not subject to the normal pharmaceutical quality controls, their efficacy must be in doubt. If you are told that the dam and other stock are given homeopathic vaccinations, ask advice from your veterinary surgeon at once as it may be that your puppy will need early protection before it leaves the breeder's premises.

When the bitches in a kennel are inoculated and boostered as necessary, the puppies receive a passive immunity via the milk produced by the dam in the first three days after whelping. If the dam died at whelping, or was unable to feed her puppies, the pups will require protection by inoculation very early, at about 3/4 weeks. This early maternally derived immunity wanes at varying ages according to the strength of antibodies in the mother's bloodstream. Puppies from a good clean kennel where the dam has been regularly boostered will be the last to need protection, as their mother's antibodies must have passed out of their system before the inoculation goes in. Too early an inoculation will be wasted. On the other hand, you will not want your new puppy to be unprotected, as the young are the most vulnerable to distemper. This is why it is important to know the date the dam was boostered, and to warn your veterinary surgeon that you intend to buy the puppy. He will then be able to advise you on the most suitable vaccine and the correct programme for use. There are several different brands and combinations to cover different contingencies, and they are all timed in a different way. There are very few puppies which will not be ready for inoculation by 12 weeks – most are ready by 8 weeks.

It is important to keep the puppy absolutely free of infection before it has the first dose of inoculation. Most cases of bad reaction to inoculation will prove to have been already incubating the disease.

Puppies in dealers' hands are often advertised as inoculated, thus making them seem a better bargain than those from an owner/breeder who has not had them done before selling. Puppies already inoculated by 8 weeks of age have almost certainly received a serum to guard against indwelling infections on the dealer's premises. Serum only gives protection for a few weeks, and you will then have to provide the normal inoculation cover as well.

If you mean to leave the puppy with the breeder until it is 10/11 weeks old, the breeder may have the first inoculation shot given for you, if you request it. You will then have to pay for the inoculation separately, and for the veterinary surgeon's visit to give it, as breeders are reluctant to take little puppies to the surgery, especially when they have a number of puppies at home. Even in the best run surgeries it is possible to pick up a virus, so we avoid the surgery for the youngest stock.

A Second Dog

If you have been very fond of a dog, you may dread the time when it dies. One way to buffer the loss is to start another puppy when the first is in late middle age. Only you can say when the right time will be, and only you will know if the original dog is capable of enjoying, or even tolerating a puppy. Certainly a really old and feeble animal should not be bothered with a bouncy puppy, but a middle aged dog may well renew its youth with a young companion. The bitch which has phantom pregnancies will receive a puppy at that time very tenderly. Most dogs will not harm a young puppy, but it is wise to allow the older dog some respite from puppy's teasing, and not to leave the two together alone until they have come to the stage of sharing a bed, which is usually indicative of a genuine animal friendship.

Preparations for the New Puppy

Fencing the garden with the utmost security is your first task. The height and durability should be more than you think will be necessary. Individuals vary very much in the height they can jump, even within a breed. Those with big shoulders and slim hindquarters usually jump better than stocky animals. Temperament also comes into it: some would never think of jumping out of their garden, and some are always planning ways of going exploring. It is wise if neighbours can be dissuaded from talking to dogs at the fence, and offering attractions to the dog. Solid fencing is better if there are dogs in adjoining gardens, otherwise they will be certain to bark at each other.

You will also need fencing and a gate to partition off the

front garden from the back, where it is assumed the dog will have its freedom. Remember dogs seem able to compress their bodies and wriggle under a small gap, so improvise protection right to the ground. Self closing catches on gates and doors will be needed. If you have handles of the press down variety, many tall dogs soon learn to open these and let themselves out, so such doors will need an internal bolt as well.

A notice on the back gate saying 'Beware of the Dog' is a good idea, even if you only have a Chihuahua puppy. It slows up callers, and prevents them flinging open gates and doors and letting the puppy out.

All members of the household should be warned that things will be different when there is a young dog in the home. Tidiness will be especially important; puppies chew up anything left about, and it will always be the fault of the human who did not protect his property. Many people feel that it is unreasonable if a puppy takes shoes or hats, because they have provided plenty of dog toys for him, but the young animal cannot really distinguish between what you mean him to have, and what it would be tempting to take. Puppies are attracted to the animal smell of leather, and to any article at all which humans have just handled, particularly humans they are fond of. This is the reason why something new, something you have only just acquired will be taken, rather than an old object which has been in the household for a long while. The blame still remains with the human who made the article accessible. Big breed puppies grow very quickly, and can soon reach up high when raised on their hind legs, so always be prepared for the pup to do just more than you expect. No main doors, or doors of bedrooms must ever be left open, and the puppy should not be allowed to wander through the house unsupervised.

You must always remember to check that the puppy is behind a closed door, before the front door is opened; so many puppies dart out and get run over. Children must be drilled into closing all doors behind them for the sake of the puppy. Special care should be taken too, when moving the car or backing into the garage, that a tiny puppy is not under the wheels where you can hardly see it. No dog should be loose when lawns are being mowed, the rotary type mower in particular can throw up stones just on the level of a dog's eyes. Do not plan to allow your puppy access to the garage, or to shut him in there any part of the day; many garage and garden substances can be poisonous to dogs, especially pools of sump oil.

If you are getting the puppy during the summer, it is wise to equip your car from the start with grilles to cover the windows, so that you may have them open without the risk of the dog putting his head out, which is obviously very dangerous. Never leave your dog in the car, even with the window and roof ventilation ajar and the car parked in the shade. A dog in a closed car, even on a cool day, can slowly cook and become desperate for oxygen. Dogs can die from heat stroke in a very short time, and in many situations the owner can be prosecuted for cruelty for leaving a dog in distress in a car.

If a previous dog has died of some infectious disease, take your veterinary surgeon's advice on the time you should wait to get another dog, and what precautions should be taken before you do. If blankets need to be washed in disinfectant, do rinse them well, as strong chemicals can cause a rash on the puppy's skin. Make sure that chemicals and bleaches normally kept in the kitchen are not accessible to the dog; sometimes puppies perform remarkable feats on undoing cupboard doors.

Swimming pools with the cover on are death traps for young dogs. If the dog runs on to the cover, he may easily fall in and be trapped, unable to get free to swim or climb out. Many puppies have drowned surprisingly quickly in this way. The only answer is to fence the pool so that the puppy has no access to this area.

Do not allow puppies to run on to ponds that are iced over. Although most dogs swim naturally, they have great difficulty in getting out if the pond sides are steep or there is only a small hole in the ice.

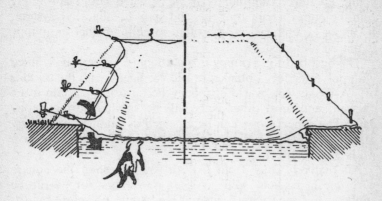

Figure 1. Sectional drawing of a pool

Tarpaulins sag and stick to the water surface

Left   A small cover carelessly fitted allows puppy to fall in the water. It will drown immediately.

Right A large cover tightly stretched and pegged down at least 45cm beyond the water surface is perfectly safe.

Provide a bed for the puppy, with soft padding. Pieces of polyester fur are ideal for the puppy's bedding (and for use in the car and over the furniture if necessary). It is a wonderful invention: cosy and warm but very easily cleaned in a washing machine. The best colour to buy, surprisingly, is white! You can then see when it is soiled or if any blood or leaking faeces appears on it. The polyester fur, which comes in a variety of brand names, will last for many years with frequent washing (even two or three times weekly). It can be bought through advertisements in the weekly dog newspapers, Dog World and Our Dogs, or through your vet.

The bed must be the puppy's own, in which he will be absolutely inviolate. Children should be warned that they must not disturb the puppy when he is asleep. Although the puppy may be willing to play, long periods of rest are essential for a young creature. Continually being agitated could absolutely ruin the puppy's temperament, and spoil his digestive system. It cannot be emphasized too often to children that the puppy is not an animated toy.

The best bed for a puppy is a cardboard grocery box, lined with polyester fur, a blanket or old cardigans with the buttons off. A basket is a waste of money because it is certain to be chewed, and most other beds will be spoiled during puppy days. The grocery box can be changed as often as necessary. Start with quite a small one, puppies like to feel the protective walls around them.

Alternatively, buy from a do-it-yourself shop the square wire mesh baskets sold to use as fittings for wardrobe cupboards. Lined with a cushion and some polyester fur (or old jumpers), these baskets make light-to-carry and easily cleaned puppy beds for every room and they have many uses once the puppy has outgrown them.

You could also profitably invest in some of the welded wire panels which are sold at do-it-yourself shops to make compost bins. These wire panels, four to a pack, are invaluable for making barriers. One at the foot of the stairs will save the puppy from running up and then tumbling headlong down. Another may be used to bar off the kitchen from the hallway, so that the puppy may see what is going on but not rush out. The panels may be fixed to doorframes with hooks.

Two bowls will be needed, one for food and one for water, both kept especially for the puppy. Water is left available always, and changed frequently. You may find you need an untippable bowl if the puppy is inclined to wade in it. Never leave the puppy's water out in the garden overnight, it could become a source of infection by contact with rat urine.

Other useful things to have by you will be a syphon of soda water, invaluable for cleaning up urine pools made by accident on the carpet. You will also need plenty of old newspaper to spread in the kitchen if you are going out. It is important for your clean-up systems to be efficient so that after

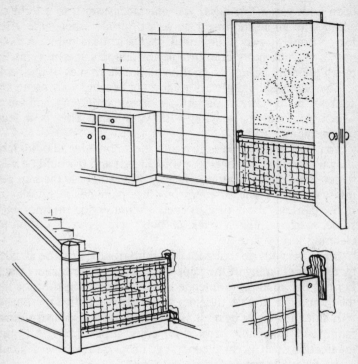

Figure 2. Frames make good barriers

Frames can be wedged across doors and stairs for easy
removal. A piece of paper against the wall protects the surface.

accidents have occurred the puppy does not return to the same
spot, as it will do if it can still recognise the smell of the place
it used before. If you are worried about this your vet will sell
you a safe system, usually consisting of floor or carpet cleaner
and a separate canister of deodorant to finish the clean up.

You will already have bought the food as directed by the
breeder. You should make no attempt to change the food for at
least two weeks.

The puppy does not need a collar and lead at first, as it will
be carried everywhere except in its own garden. After it has

been with you a few days, you may accustom it to a light cat collar with an elastic insert, to be worn only when supervised for an hour or two a day, until it gets to be a habit. A body harness can be more comfortable for puppies and prevents too much pressure being put on the vulnerable tissues of the neck.

The puppy should always wear a tag bearing your name and address, or the correct particulars of any temporary address at which you may be staying with your dog. This is a legal requirement.

You will need grooming tools (your breeder should have shown you what you need for your breed) and it would be wise to get some puppy shampoo from your vet in case the pup gets infested with rabbit fur mites or other parasites when playing in the garden. You will also need a blunt ended thermometer, some vaseline, and a pack of baby wipes (very useful for cleaning puppy faces).

Many vets advise that a lot of mouth troubles can be avoided by regular cleaning of the puppy's teeth from the earliest stage. Do not use toothpaste intended for humans; dogs do not like the foaming action. A medium grade short-handled toothbrush will suit the puppy best. It is possible to buy meat-flavoured toothpaste, especially created for dogs, at pet shops. All other medication such as ear-cleaner, eye drops and wormers should come from the vet.

There are a couple of other things which it is also useful to have. Buy from the chemist a bottle of gripe water as intended for human babies. Your puppy will almost certainly get hiccoughs from time to time after eating and a teaspoonful of gripe water eases the situation very quickly. Some milk of magnesia tablets are also useful to have in case the puppy gets tummy rumbles or other signs of indigestion.

Finally, you will probably also want some toys for your puppy, and in this context I urge you to buy some toys which are designed for dogs, not designed to amuse humans as so many of the light plastic toys made as caricatures of famous people really are. Make sure the toy is of hard rubber or bone-hard nylon, then it will stand up to the rigorous chewing most puppies give their toys. Another favourite is a length of rope for tug-of-war games.

Balls must be large enough not to get wedged in the back of the throat, so you will have to move on in size as the puppy grows. Enthusiastic catching and keeping the ball has resulted in too many fatalities, so dispose of any outgrown ball at once. If the puppy does get a ball stuck in the back of the mouth, do not attempt to remove it from the front, as the saliva produced by a choking dog will prevent your action being effective. The best method is to get behind the dog, and to grasp the cheekbones on the outside of the face and push forward, thereby dislodging the ball.

A furry cuddly toy can be a lot of fun and also a comfort, but do make sure to remove any eyes or other ornaments which may come off easily. Do not give as a toy anything in plastic which may be chewed up or where the squeaker is easy to extract. Proper dog toys are surprisingly expensive but will last for many years and be really well played with.

What you do not need

Anything elaborate or delicate in the way of beds or bedding. Any chocolate drops or sweets, it is a pity to accustom the pup to sugar taste.

Any condition powders, or vitamin preparations, apart from those on the feeding chart given you. Considerable harm can be done by overdosage with vitamins; and the well fed, well cared for puppy will be in splendid condition without extra aid.

8.

The Puppy in Your Home

It is a good idea to explore your house from a puppy's viewpoint before he arrives, crawling around with your head about 20cm from the floor. This will bring sharply into focus all the interesting things you could pull at and destroy if you really were a puppy. It is certainly a salutary exercise. Make sure that your kitchen cupboards have dog-proof fastenings. Apart from gorging on the contents of your store cupboard, your puppy may get at poisonous liquids in the cleaning cupboard.

If possible, replace any old lead-based paint on doors and skirtings with a modern paint which does not contain lead. Puppies often chew at woodwork and paint containing lead is a lethal substance. (If your puppy becomes really addicted to chewing wood, it may be useful to protect corners with metal angle-strip and to put a sheet of perspex over doors temporarily.)

Many dogs find out how to open refrigerator doors which close with a magnetic catch. Your puppy will not be able to do this until he is older, but many dog-owning homes have to keep the fridge door chained up when their dog learns this trick.

While checking on the kitchen, look at electrical connections and in particular trailing flexes. Shorten all connections as much as you can, and try to make them inaccessible. The same applies to the washing machine hose... this can be a favourite chew-object. It is probably wise to turn the electric current off at the mains when you leave the dog in the kitchen while you are out. The switches on electric hotplates are easily turned on by investigating paws, and a red-hot ceramic hob could be the means of starting a fire.

Fit all your room heaters with fire-guards; puppies will scorch their fur and their skin by leaning against even an enclosed electric fire, so you need a projecting guard which keeps them well away.

House Training

When you first arrive home don't put the puppy down; it is sure to want to urinate after the journey, so carry it straight to the garden. House training starts now. You have a good portent in knowing the puppy is likely to want to perform, so wait with it until it does, and then encourage and congratulate it, meanwhile saying your particular euphemism for the action. Decide on one phrase and stick to it. Quite soon the puppy will begin to associate the action with your words, but not if you continually vary your words. In dog training it is important to keep all words as short as possible, with crisp sounds. Always use the same words with no extra embellishments. We say 'Go and be good', others use 'Hurry Up!' It is very useful if your dog will, in later life, perform on command.

If the weather is very bad, and you have taken a six week old puppy, you may need to spread newspaper on the kitchen or loggia floor for the pup to use until it is old enough to be taken outside. Successful and rapid house training depends entirely on how much time the owner can give to the task, and it can be an almost full time occupation for several months.

Learn to read the puppy's body language and indications that he wants to go and be ready to take him outside quickly. The logistics of your house are important here; you and the puppy must spend your days in a room with an easy exit to outside. Always take the puppy out when he rouses from sleep in the day time, you will almost certainly get pleasing results at that time so you can praise lavishly and the message of "being good" will get home all the sooner.

You may notice the puppy sniffing about on the carpet in an urgent manner, or maybe staring at the door where he usually goes out. Baby animals do not give much warning, so you have to be prepared to drop whatever you are doing. If you are not available to attend the puppy's needs, then an accident is entirely your fault. It's tough but true!

You must be prepared to stay outside with the puppy until you get results, as taking it outside may distract the butterfly mind of a young animal from its primary purpose. Walk about with the pup, saying your "words" and giving praise when you get results. We say "oh, she's so clever!" which seems to work. It is of no use to dump the pup outside and close the door on him, that teaches nothing at all and will induce no association between going outside and elimination.

The young puppy has very little control of its functions, and at first, lapses must be forgiven to the dog and blamed on the person who was not quick enough to see what was about to be done.

If there are difficulties about getting the puppy outside quickly it is useful to make a regime of "every hour on the hour". Urination is as frequent as this in puppies, but faeces are usually passed only after a meal. Wake the puppy for the hourly exit if it is asleep during the day, so as not to break the routine. Yes, it all takes a great deal of concentration but think how much more quickly the pup is trained to be self sufficient compared with the human infant! The vast majority of pups will be completely house trained by the age of nine months, the human will take four times as long.

Do not allow the puppy free run of your home, where there is the opportunity to soil carpets and ruin upholstery. Keep him in an easily cleaned room unless you have him under strict supervision.

Most puppies are trained to use pads of newspaper by their breeders, and this may be your best method over night, but it is best avoided during the day time unless you must leave the puppy alone. The longer you continue with newspaper by day, the harder it is to train the puppy to use the garden.

When the puppy is to some extent house trained, he will still have some back-slidings when left too long, or if he gets excited during play. You may express your regret, but you do not punish, because it is absolutely no use doing so. Rubbing his nose in it is old-fashioned, cruel and senseless. House training depends on the owners, and there are very few dogs who do not get the hang of it in time. If a dog is kennelled or shut in a room for a long time, he will have no choice but to soil the floor. Dogs seldom bark to ask to go out; they will indicate their need in many ways, but only if you are looking and available.

Bladder control at night is quite hard to acquire, especially if you are not early risers. If you can get the puppy out at first light, it helps. Directly the puppy is roused he will want to go out, you cannot even afford to wait until you have put the kettle on. If you get persistent soiling at night when the puppy is getting older, you may want to consider altering the feeding pattern so that the last meal is given earlier and the puppy has time to empty himself before bedtime. Sometimes if you are giving a milky meal at night it may be useful to reverse the order and give a solid meal last thing.

Fresh water should be always available wherever the puppy is. Do not be tempted to withhold water because the puppy urinates during the night. It is a major cruelty to do this.

Puppies who appear to be otherwise very well and happy are often struck with diarrhoea after a few hours or more in the new home. I think this must be entirely due to nerves and tension which will be present even if the puppy seems to be having fun. Reduce the amounts fed for one day; cuddle the puppy and give it quiet affection, not noisy play or rough handling.

Puppy meals

The puppy will now be ready for his first meal in your home. Feed everything at room temperature, never straight from the refrigerator. The puppy may not eat as much as the breeder predicted, either because it is distracted by new things, or because there is no longer the competitive element of brothers and sisters. Do not worry, appetite will soon be regained. The first meal should be left on the floor for about 10 minutes and then removed. Do not allow the puppy to pick at his food and wander about, coming back for another mouthful or two. Keep the room quiet at this time, do not interrupt while the pup is eating.

If the food is left, do not offer more until the next feeding time, but be sure to keep to a regular timetable. Take the puppy to the garden after every meal and when it wakes from sleep. After the meal and the garden visit, have a little play time. Let the puppy set the pace, do not over excite, and when energy flags, show it the bed you have provided. Then let the puppy sleep as long as it wants to without interference. Puppies drop suddenly from intense activity to utter exhaustion.

Although you are naturally proud of your puppy, it would be wise not to ask people in to see it during the first few days with you. Let it adjust to the new home and family first.

You will not be able to have visiting dogs in your house or garden until after the whole course of puppy inoculations is through. After its first sleep in your home, you may start to teach the puppy its name, or if you have not decided, call 'puppy'. The next important word is NO! said very sharply, whenever he does something that is forbidden. Use the one word, consistently, to re-inforce the message. At this stage you should not apply any punishment, just provide a distraction by offering something else, but later, if he should be defiant, the NO! may be re-inforced with a slap, given at the moment of commission of an error ONLY. This is what the dam, or pack leader would do. You too can use the growly voice of a mature dog, and if necessary, hold the pup's head to the ground in a gesture of submission.

Calculated punishment long after the event is of no use to the dog as a lesson, and merely degrades you.

If something has happened that the dog could not help, such as a pool in the kitchen when you are late getting up, or a book torn which was left just where he could get it, I find it better to ignore the episode. I feel it is important for your relationship with the dog that it should consider you just and reasonable. Some dogs will never need any physical correction — a harsh voice is as much as they can bear. Other harder characters, particularly in the males, will sometimes have to be shown that you are the bigger animal.

The first night

I am probably going to ask you to break all the rules you have agreed on. I think if you acquire a young puppy it is asking too much to expect it to stay alone at night in a strange house, away from brothers and sisters for the first time. Dogs are naturally creatures which value body contact and huddling together; they gain security and warmth from each other, and it is natural for them to turn to the pack when they feel threatened. I have learnt that it is asking too much of this little pup which has been so bold all day, undergoing its first journey and all these new experiences in your home, to stay alone all night in unfamiliar surroundings. My advice to you is to take the pup in its box into your bedroom, or sleep downstairs with it, for one or two weeks, until you and the house are absolutely familiar. Sleeping with people need not become a habit of a lifetime, because when the dog is fully integrated with your family, and is more active all day, you can start training him to stay alone at night wherever you have decided will make warm, draught-free sleeping quarters. Training will be easier at this stage as you will have already started leaving the pup for short periods in the daytime, and he is not going to be panicked by strangeness.

The advantages of having the puppy beside your bed are that you can comfort it if it is lonely in the night, and that you have more control over house training, as you can take the pup out immediately it stirs.

You can of course make your puppy stay alone on the first night, and go and shout at it every time it cries, as it undoubtedly will, but I do not think this is the best foundation for a long and trusting friendship, or for a calm and confident pet, who is afraid of nothing because he was reared in security. Your aim should be to make the puppy look on you as the pack leader who provides shelter and comfort, as his dam did. He cries in protest to call the pack to him: and what do you do? Inflict punishment for wholly natural behaviour, or reassure him that he has a new pack now, and that you and he will jointly protect each other? I feel that many of the problems that people have with dogs who can never be left alone, or who are always hysterical and jittery, may well stem from a terrifying experience early in the relationship and a lack of sympathy from the new owners from which the puppy may never recover confidence. The puppy has already crammed a lot of experience into a few weeks of life; do not demand too much too soon, and you will have a more satisfactory companion in the end.

Things that may worry you
1. Teething
One of the first events to be gone through with a new puppy is the teething stage, which starts at about 12 weeks of age and goes on until about 18 weeks.

During this stage the puppy does feel some discomfort, or perhaps frank pain, and this is usually taken out on human hands. The need to bite very hard is compulsive, and it seems at times that only human flesh will satisfy this need; toys and sticks are no use at all to the puppy. So your hands will suffer, but take comfort that this stage will come to an end when the second teeth are through the gums. There seems no way to soothe the puppy's pain. I once bought some baby teething jelly to rub on the gums but the puppy ate a tube a day and I had no proof that it did any good.

Some new owners may feel that this juvenile hand biting

may indicate that the puppy will be fierce or a danger to children. Emphatically, this is not so. Older people complain of this phase the most, because hands with fine skin and prominent veins do bruise easily and small abrasions take longer to heal.

2. The puppy is eating its own faeces, or the manure of other animals. This habit which we find so objectionable is a fact of life to many animals including dogs, especially at the puppy stage when they are used to their dam clearing up after them.

Watchfulness is the great preventer here. Pick up and dispose of the pup faeces directly they are passed, and keep a sharp watch on walks, shouting "NO" at once if you see the puppy investigating rabbit or deer droppings. This habit of faeces eating is not as prevalent as it once was, as dogs fed on the modern complete dried diets pass faeces which are low in bulk and which seem to have very little attraction for re-consumption.

Disposal of faeces

The excreta from one pet dog may be picked up in soft paper and disposed of in the household sewerage system. Alternatively, you can pick up with a plastic bag inverted over your gloved hand, turn the bag inside out and deposit inside a plastic carrier which can be tied up and put with the household waste. It is not a good idea to put dog (or cat) faeces on the compost heap, since if any toxocara canis worms have been passed the heating-up process of the compost heap will be an ideal breeding ground for them and you may be distributing them again in your garden. For the same reason it is not wise to dig dog and cat faeces into the soil. Dispose of these waste products as permanently as possible.

Bleached circles on the lawn

This is inevitable, on some types of ground, if you keep a bitch and train her to urinate on grass. She could be trained to use paving or concrete. If she uses the grass the only way to prevent the lawn being ruined is to pour two or three gallons of water on to the urine pool immediately. Lawns based on chalk soil do not seem to mark as badly.

Eating stones

Most puppies seem to delight in picking up stones and almost inevitably some get swallowed. Puppies seem to be able to get away with taking down a fair handful of gravel but once in a while a larger piece will cause an obstruction in the intestine and your veterinary surgeon will have to operate in order to remove it because the puppy will be in serious pain. If you see your dog with a stone in its mouth do not dive upon it with the object of taking the stone, as the dog will sometimes swallow it deliberately to prevent you getting possession. Offer a biscuit or a sweet, and as the dog takes the titbit, hook your finger into the mouth and flip the stone out. Another veterinary bill saved!

9.

Training a Puppy

The first weeks

After two or three days in your home, you may begin to accustom the puppy to spending short periods alone, say 10 minutes while you go into another room. Perhaps you will darken the room where the puppy is first to simulate night. If the pup starts to wail at the door, give a couple of bangs from outside and say 'Lie Down', 'Be Quiet', whatever your phrase is to be, in the low growly voice. Do not add any other words or the pup will keep calling you back for a chat. You can work up to half an hour quite soon, then to an hour while you are shopping; only very rarely should it be for longer in puppy days. Tidy up before you close the door and remove anything likely to be damaged. Take out the plugs of electrical apparatus and see the leads are hung high above puppy reach.

Remember to praise the puppy extravagantly when you go back if he has managed well, and growl and grumble if he has not. Slaps only work if he is caught in the act, never for something done even a few minutes ago. The dog has not the type of brain to associate misdeeds with deferred punishment.

If the puppy has been left alone but subject to some

disturbance such as someone at the door or the telephone, it may be understandable that he has done some damage in an effort to get to the callers. This is particularly true in the guarding breeds who feel frustrated when they hear noise they cannot identify.

Lead training can start in the garden at the end of the pup's first week with you. Practise only for a few minutes at a time, never allowing the puppy to pull. Lead training is very important, especially among the stronger breeds, as it will form an important component towards the success of your partnership with the dog. Do not allow children to pull a puppy around on a lead; they are likely to give a pup all the wrong ideas on lead training, and if they are too forceful, may frighten or even injure a puppy by too strong pressure on the neck. Lead training must be taken seriously; just encourage and restrain until you have the pup moving steadily at your side without any tension on the lead. Puppies learn best with a light collar and separate lead. Check or choke chains are now very much out of favour, as it has been found that jerking on the chain can do very serious harm to the larynx and the throat. Do not be persuaded into any kind of chain neckware; you can train your dog to behave well without cruel equipment.

Do make sure that the pup walks just at your side; so many owners settle for just 6 inches in front, which will become a tiresome tug when the dog is older. Sometimes the puppy will take the lead in its mouth; this is usually an aid to getting it along, and can be cured when the basic idea has been taught. Once the puppy has had a few days to adjust to you, it is possible to start teaching a few other words like 'SIT'.

It is convenient to have a little teaching session just before meals, when the puppy's attention is on you anyway. Say, 'Puppy, sit', meanwhile pushing the hindquarters down, and holding for a few seconds. Teaching the puppy to come to your call is very important. Use his name often, call him and fuss and praise him, so that he thinks it is a very special thing to come to you. If you call him frequently for nothing more than a little conversation and affection, he will not associate being called with having to be shut in, or stopping something enjoyable. It is not wise to start a routine of food rewards for coming, or you will never be able to stop.

Never chase a puppy as a game or because he is tantalising you by not coming to your call. The odds will be in the pup's favour of being the faster and the more agile, and trying to catch a laughing puppy is very frustrating and could lead you both into danger if it takes place outside the garden. The best thing to do is walk *away;* very deflating to the pup, who will find it more convenient to follow you in the end. Children should not chase a puppy as a game as it only leads to bad habits.

Try to avoid the puppy jumping up to attract your attention; get down to his level instead. With the large, heavy breeds it is useful to establish a ritual for welcoming people in which the dog brings a toy, or is given a glove to carry off. This turns off the overwhelming exuberance which they feel at greeting friends and owners.

Many veterinary surgeons now run puppy classes, where pups which have had their first preventative vaccinations can meet other puppies, and learn to be handled by other owners, the vets themselves and their nurses. Meanwhile, while the puppies play, the vet will hold a simple instruction class about various aspects of puppy care. These classes have proved very successful in accustomising puppies to the atmosphere and the smells at the veterinary surgery, and also in acclimatizing them to other dogs, and other people. The cost is usually minimal and owners enjoy it too!

Most puppies do not require any formal exercise for four to five months. Too much sustained exercise can easily overtire the pup and put strain on growing joints. Garden exercise, and being played with, together with a short run in an open space is quite enough until five months of age.

It is a good idea to formulate your play with the dog according to his natural abilities. Teach the gundog to retrieve a pair of rolled up socks, the hound to find a concealed article.

This gives the dog mental occupation, and stimulates his natural talent. Tug-of-war, provided the human does not exert too much power, is excellent for Bull breeds, and develops strong fronts and neck. Do not play this game with a gundog, which should always give up an article quickly and cleanly.

You will probably be interested in taking your dog to a training class to teach him to obey amid the maximum temptations of other dogs and other people. You are sure to see a class advertised in the pet columns of local newspapers or in the veterinary surgery. It is as well to get the puppy's name down early, so that he can start training at six months; the minimum age for most classes. Most courses close down during the Summer months and resume in the Autumn term. Charges are very small, and many owners enjoy the social contact with other people interested in dogs. Basic training should have been begun before the class, as it is not the place to wrestle with a dog which is wearing a collar for the first time.

Car travel should be continued at every opportunity, so that it becomes second nature to the dog. Many owners like to carry the puppy down a busy shopping street at quite an early age, so the puppy may see and hear all the bustle of life, while feeling secure and unthreatened in the owner's arms.

Grooming should be begun in the first week you have the pup in the manner shown you by the breeder. Apart from keeping the coat healthy and free from tangle, the grooming session allows you close contact with the dog, and an opportunity to feel all over for lumps and bumps which may indicate trouble. Insist that the dog endures with patience. Pick up the feet separately, open the mouth, clean the ears, take a quick look at the anal glands. A dog that will allow complete examination wins friends and saves expensive time at the vet's surgery. It may also save having an anaesthetic for minor treatments if the animal is willing to be handled.

Most treatments and repair work available for humans are

now being performed for dogs. Because this can be very expensive it is wise to insure against veterinary fees. You can then allow the vet to go ahead with any operation or drug treatment necessary without worrying about the cost. Many insurances also cover against any damage caused to property or people by your puppy.

10.

Beware of the Dangers

Young puppies have very little reserves of stamina and body weight, so that if they become ill they need veterinary attention rather more quickly than does the adult dog. As with a human, some conditions in the adult bear waiting a day or two, keeping the animal quiet and warm without exercise, to see how the illness resolves, but puppies will want diagnosis after one day of being poorly. You will use your discretion as you would with a human child in assessing the degree of illness, taking into account the number and severity of the symptoms. Dogs have no more recuperative powers than humans, so that if you find your puppy is ill, you must get it treated before complications develop.

The sick dog is listless, dull, disinclined to play. He will retire to his bed and suffer in silence. Only you can say how different his behaviour is from normal, and that will be the biggest clue you can give your veterinary surgeon.

You will realise that diagnosis of illness in animals, and the provision of the right treatment straight away, depends very much on the information and history that the owner can give, and only relatively little on the symptoms indicated by the dog. Most symptoms, like raised temperature, loss of appetite, vomiting, indicate nearly all canine diseases. You provide the other clues which can lead the vet to pinpoint the likely cause.

New puppies are their own worst enemies for picking up and eating what they should not, so it is as well to search your mind for the happenings of the day or two days before the dog became ill.

Puppies chew on all sorts of things, and many ordinary plants we have in our gardens can be poisonous. You may need to put a wire fence around them until the pup loses interest in stealing plants. Bulbs like daffodil, tulip and crocus, and also lilies will cause an internal upset, and even excitement, collapse and coma; so keep the puppy away when you are planting and watch that he is not digging up bulbs to chew. There is a great fascination in retrieving something you have just put into the earth. Buttercup, foxglove, larkspur and peony leaves and flowers are dangerous, too. Green leaves of potato and tomato, and shrubs like azalea, wisteria and privet must never be chewed either. Laburnum seeds and fallen sticks are, again, dangerous if chewed, as is the green Leyland Cyprus which borders so many gardens. The latter will also bring up a rash if the puppy rolls about in hedge trimmings. I do not think that puppies are very attracted to these plants, but they may take a branch when you are pruning, or chew the shrub beside the back door.

Christmas can be a special danger time for puppies because the traditional decorations, holly berries, yew branches, mistletoe berries and poinsettia leaves, are poisonous to dogs. Keep them well out of reach.

Many dogs will interfere with houseplants, whether as a substitute for grass, or just from sheer mischief. Poinsettia, Mother-in-Law's Tongue, Philodendron and Bleeding Heart stems and leaves cause swelling of mouth and throat tissues, and could bring about death by choking in a small puppy, or a dog with a short face, like the Pug and Boxer.

Fallen apples are very attractive to play with but may have been contaminated by rats. No effective mouse and rat killer is safe for dogs; the effects are cumulative, so any dog that is seen to touch rat bait should go at once to a vet for an injection of Vitamin K1. Take care when walking your dog around barns and haystacks in the country; the rat man lays his poison there, and the dog may find it before you are aware. Dead mice, rats and birds are a risk; they may have been poisoned, and the dog should never have them to play with. Lead paint is an acute poison; sometimes old doors are used to barricade areas from the puppy, and if these are chewed there is quite enough lead to make the dog acutely ill, perhaps fatally. There is also lead in lino, and golf balls — these are also too small for most puppies to play with safely; too small a ball is easily swallowed in excitement.

Slug bait can never be used in a dog owner's garden, as it is absolutely deadly to dogs, and they do seem to be attracted to it. If you are using any weed killer, I advise keeping the dog in at least until it has dried on the leaves. Artificial fertilizers and lawn dressings need to be very carefully used too, and the dog kept away. Remember that the puppy does not have to eat any, he can get a large quantity just by cleaning it off his paws.

Farm weedkillers are very much stronger than those sold to the public, and if they are being sprayed behind a tractor, they may be carried a long way on the wind, and get ingested from coat and paws. Contact with weedkiller can give a bad dose of diarrhoea after a country walk. Eating cow and horse manure will also cause bowel looseness, but this should clear up when the irritant substance has been passed. Dogs are very attracted to manure, whether on the rosebeds or found in a field. Keep your dog on a lead in the cow field unless you are prepared to have a dirty kitchen floor that night.

Never allow your dog to drink from stagnant lakes or pools. Some freshwater algae are very poisonous, and will kill within hours of the dog taking a drink. Running moorland streams are usually fine for wading in, and drinking from.

At home, please use all disinfectants in the correct measured strength; too strong a chemical can cause minor burns on muzzle and paws, and inflammation in the eyes. Take great care with antiseptic aerosol sprays too; the alcohol propellant can burn a puppy's eyes. Cakes and bars of soap are very attractive to the dog, because of the fat content. If the soap foams up in the dog's mouth, he may choke before you can help him. Use only liquid soap in the kitchen, and keep the bathroom door closed. Big breed puppies have been known to take a drink from a lavatory which contained corrosive cleaner. They will also take a lick from your scrubbing bucket. If you suspect that a puppy has had a minute quantity of a burning substance, a drink of milk is a quick soother, and may avert damage by diluting the poison; of course, this does not work if a significant amount has been taken.

Anti-freeze and sump oil present hazards in the garage; keep the dog out. Some types of water and central heating apparatus can give off toxic fumes just at dog level; do not shut a dog in a cupboard or a small space with a boiler. Watch out for gas taps and electric wiring, and also telephone wire, which is not dangerous but you will find it very annoying to have your phone cut off by the puppy. Never leave the collar on a dog when it is alone in kitchen or car, as it could catch on a projecting handle and cause asphyxiation; this is not an uncommon type of accident. Two dogs playing together should not wear loose collars either, as one may get its teeth hooked in the other's collar and be caused intense pain.

The last warning is about scalds and burns through cooking splashes. Dogs are better out of the way during frying and jam making. If you feel you may have splashed the dog but cannot see any harm done, do search right into the coat; sometimes the hair will fall out several days later, revealing a blister on the underlying skin.

All accidents should be shown to a veterinary surgeon, especially falls and bangs by a car from which the puppy seems to recover quickly, in case some internal damage has been done.

Illness

Probably the very first taste you will have of a less than 100% well puppy will be at about 10 days after the first shot of a distemper inoculation. Many little dogs experience a day when they are not very lively, refuse to eat and want to lie in their beds. Take care of him, especially do not overtire him or let him be cold. He should be back to normal next day; if not, he needs the vet. This small reaction to the inoculation indicates that antibodies are being formed and the vaccination has taken. Provided recovery has taken place in 24 hours it is nothing to worry about. Just occasionally, the vaccination against hepatitis will affect the eyes. If you find a blue film appearing over one or both eyes, you need to tell the vet at once. Do not treat in any way with drops or ointments. Other types of sore or discharging eyes may be caused by irritations, perhaps tobacco smoke if the puppy has never experienced it before. Get the right type of drops from the vet.

Canine Parvovirus

This killer virus was a completely new disease in dogs in 1979, and many dogs died before it was recognised and before safe vaccines were established. Now the disease is largely under control, thanks to efficient vaccination, but there are still periodic outbreaks in refuges which take unwanted or stray dogs and also in big cities.

CPV shows as serious, blood-filled diarrhoea accompanied by deep depression and collapse. Notify your vet at once if you suspect CPV and ask what you should do. The dog may need to be given fluid intravenously and you should regard your home as out of bounds to other dogs and dog owners. CPV virus can be transmitted from infected premises on shoes and clothing for up to a year, but the virus is killed on floors and walls by the application of household bleach.

CPV vaccination regimes are now very good, but there will always be some dogs which do not respond to vaccination. If you are worried as to the vulnerability of your puppy, your vet can arrange to send a bloodtest to a laboratory to ascertain the level of protection your puppy has.

11.

Care of the Puppy

Ears

Ears soon begin to smell if they are dirty, and quickly make a dog undesirable. Accumulated wax, or an overgrowth of hair in the ears, forms an ideal place for ear mites to multiply. Keep ears clean by putting in a drop or two of warm almond oil with a dropper, and gently cleaning as far as you can see with cotton wool. Never probe with a cotton bud. For breeds that dangle their ears in their food, improvise a stocking cap to be worn while eating. If you can see a brown discharge in the ear, get veterinary advice before it gets acute. Scratching of the ears, especially if a little yelp is given, indicates trouble. Keep spaniel ears combed free, and remove any knots and burrs daily before they become matted in. Ears form a comfortable home for lice around the edges, probably needing a special wash with shampoo from the vet.

Many shops sell dog remedies, medicines and shampoos, but if the condition you are out to cure is anything other than a cosmetic one, it is much better to go to a veterinary surgeon and have the correct substance prescribed, rather than waste money on some unspecific remedy which may be sold freely over the counter. The most effective remedies are on prescription only.

Teeth

Puppies get their second and permanent teeth between 4 and 5 months of age. You may find the baby teeth shed on the floor, and the puppy may be desperate to chew something at this time. Inspect the mouth regularly to ensure that all the baby teeth do come out and are not obstructing the way of a second tooth. Sometimes one will have to be removed by the vet.

Feet

The puppy will have had its nails clipped regularly by the breeder, but they will be getting too tough by the time you receive the pup for you to go on cutting them with scissors. With nail clippers it is very easy to take too much off and cut the quick, which is very painful indeed. I prefer that nails should be worn down by running on concrete, gravel or beach, or our local flint-strewn ground. Road walking keeps the feet nice and tight. A dog continually exercised on soft ground will have spread paws, but this does not matter except in the case of the show dog.

Many owners like to wipe the dog's feet when he comes in from the garden, and he may be taught to stand on the door mat and give each paw in turn. Never use disinfectant solution on the feet with an idea of preventing germs; you can cause a rash and infect the nail bed. If yours is a breed in which it is customary to leave the dew claws (equivalent to human thumb, just above the foot), keep an eye to see that they do not grow round in a circle and penetrate the leg, causing a painful ulcer. Many continental sheepdog breeds keep the claws on, other types of dog have them removed at 3/4 days old if it is customary in the breed.

Coats

Most puppies have a soft coat which is longer and fluffier than the adult one. This baby coat will be shed, and the right texture coat should be through at about six months, often in a different shade from the puppy hair. When the adult coat is coming in, the pup will look a bit patchy; extra grooming will get rid of the baby coat fast. Some dogs shed hair all the year round, the medium coats like corgis and labradors are examples. Longer haired dogs lose a significant amount of coat in Spring and Autumn, but the practice of centrally heating houses has given dogs a tendency to shed hair to some extent all the year. Coats that have become dry, and scurfy skins, can be improved by the addition of a little vegetable oil to the dog's food.

Always use a special dog shampoo for bathing your dog; it is formulated differently from those for human hair. Never use detergent liquid or powder on your dog. If they have got themselves very dirty, they may be sponged down with warm water and dried well. Unless dogs are being shown they should not want bathing more than twice a year if they are groomed and brushed daily.

Tail Ends

Around the anus of a dog are two 'anal glands'. If the dog has been constipated these glands can become enlarged, and inflamed to a bright pink, clearly visible when he is excreting. The glands will emit a foul smell, noticeable when you are sitting with him in the evening. There is a breed tendency to impacted anal glands, and if you find they are giving trouble, the veterinary surgeon can evacuate them for you.

Male dogs sometimes have an excess of hair on the sheath of the penis, which will become soaked in urine and emit a smell. You may gently trim some of the hair off, but not too closely. The male puppy will urinate in a squatting position, as the bitch does, for his first year, not attaining the male pose with the lifted leg until he is adult. Males sometimes have a drop or two of creamy discharge from this penis, this is quite normal.

Young male dogs, at about the age of 6 months, often have an excess of sexual drive, when they have become over-excited in play, which will lead them to practise mounting and mating behaviour with cushions, or people's legs. This stage seldom persists; it would seem to be caused by an imbalance of hormone secretion during adolescence. The pet dog is easy to distract, with some titbit or more constructive play, and you will find this phase will pass. A dog intended for stud work should not be shouted at or forbidden from simulated mounting, or he may be difficult to encourage when you want him to perform with a bitch.

A dog that persists in unwanted mating behaviour with inanimate objects or on people's legs is objectionable, but fortunately this behaviour pattern can be successfully altered by hormone treatment from the veterinary surgeon.

Fleas, Lice and Ticks

Even with the greatest care, it is difficult to prevent your puppy picking up fleas, but you can prevent him becoming infested. Hedgehogs, clumps of nettles and long grass harbour parasites, so it is inevitable that fleas will alight on the dog. Some breeds have a peculiar chemistry which seems to attract more parasites than do other breeds. You will find traces of flea excreta, like fine black dust in the coat − just in front of the root of the tail is a favoured place. If you quickly turn the dog onto his back, you may see a flea or two scuttle away into the warm folds of the groin.

Many respectable homes harbour a huge flea population because fleas breed and spend most of the time not on the dog, but around the edges of fitted carpets and in upholstered furniture.

There are now comprehensive programmes of anti-flea ammunition which your vet can supply; usually one type of spray for use on the furnishings and one for use on the dog. Make sure you use the right one for its particular purpose, but to be most effective the house and all the animals there-in, including the cat, should be treated on the same day, so there is maximum kill for the fleas.

These flea killers need to be treated with respect, so be sure to buy them at the veterinary surgery where you will be given the most suitable preparations for your need. Cheaper sprays purchased elsewhere may not be as effective, and since every flea left in a warm home may produce hundreds more within a few weeks, it is important that you eradicate the enemy as effectively and as quickly as possible.

Some dogs are allergic to the bite of just one flea, and so they may be scratching at a rash long after the flea has passed on. This situation needs veterinary advice or a major longlasting skin infection can result.

I do not favour the so-called anti-flea collars. It seems wrong to put a source of a strong chemical so close to the dog's eyes, nose and mouth, and I do not think flea collars are safe where there are young children.

Lice are seen with the naked eye as tiny white beads which do not move, they are attached to hair, often on the edge of the ears. An anti-parasitical wash is the best answer.

Ticks, the size of a small brown seed, embed themselves in the dog's skin where they will suck blood until they enlarge into pea or bean size, when they will drop off, making a blood stain on your carpet.

Ticks cause the dog very little irritation and seem to do no harm unless the dog has a massive infestation, possibly from rolling on grass where sheep are kept. You can pull the tick out *by the head,* using fine tweezers, where the head enters the skin, cleaning the site with alcohol afterwards.

Worming

It is essential, both as a social necessity and for the health of your dog, that he should be wormed frequently as a puppy and at six monthly intervals afterwards. All puppies have a burden of roundworm (toxocara canis) in their intestines. The worms themselves die when they are voided in faeces but they will already have laid their eggs, which are invisible and shed in their hundreds in the faeces of unwormed dogs.

The eggs can take many months to mature into the larval stage, by which time all traces of the faeces in which they were deposited have vanished. Therefore the fear which many people have of the danger of dog faeces is actually unwarranted, as the larvae may be disseminated in wind and rain and so be very far from where it was deposited by the time it matures to the larval stage which may, very rarely, infect children if they chance to swallow a larva through licking fingers or sucking grass. Most of the larvae, if swallowed, will be killed by our very strong stomach acids, but in a very few cases the larvae may get into the blood stream and may lodge in an organ of the body, such as an eye, causing some loss of sight. This is a regrettable and very sad situation but it is not a reason for getting rid of all dogs!

Puppies must be wormed frequently, with effective wormers, as advised by your vet. Modern wormers do not require any prior starvation; they are easy to administer, often being given with food, and the worms are re-digested in the dog so that you do not see any worms passed, but if the dose was properly calculated, the greatest part of the worm burden will have been eradicated. The eggs which remain in the dog will still mature, so worming must be done at regular intervals to ensure that our dogs are as worm-free and safe to be with as we can possibly make them.

There are three points to remember in the face of any criticism.

1. Your dog is regularly treated for roundworm and so is as free from risk as a living animal can be.

2. Freshly passed dog faeces on the pavement is unpleasant, but not a risk of infection to humans at this stage. All the same, you always "pick-up" after your dog as it is anti-social not to do so.

3. The thread worms which infest so many young children in nursery schools are a completely different species of worm, and *nothing to do with dogs!* Thread worm eggs are passed from child to child and are not transferred to dogs and cats or vice-versa.

Identification

Many people feel that they would like their puppy permanently identified as theirs, as an aid to getting the dog back if it is lost or stolen.

It is recommended to have the puppy "Identichipped", that is to have a small electronic device inserted into the skin at the back of the dog's neck. A veterinary surgeon will do this for you and forward the dog's particulars and yours to the National Dog Register. The chip can be read by a special 'reading device' which many dog homes and police stations now possess. The Identichip lasts for life and does not affect the dog at all.

Another method of semi-permanent identification is for a number to be tattooed on the dog's inner thigh or in the ear, but in time the number can become obscured.

12.

Not Very Well?

Veterinary surgeons care for all an animal's needs. They act as dentist, optician, surgeon and midwife. Most have in-patient facilities for keeping very sick animals and they have qualified veterinary nurses to look after them. X-rays, operations and other treatments take place on the vet's premises; there is no equivalent of the NHS District Hospitals where human patients go for emergency treatment and surgery.

There is a growing number of veterinary surgeons in private practice who have acquired post-graduate qualifications in one or more specialities, such as dermatology, ophthalmology and orthopaedics. If your dog's problems seem to be difficult to resolve you are within your rights to ask to be referred to an appropriate specialist, either in private practice or at a veterinary college. You must be referred by a general practitioner vet.

Changing Veterinary Practices

There are many reasons why you may want to change to another practice, and it is perfectly possible to do so, since you are the paying customer. It is most tactful to change when your

dog is well, and not in the middle of a course of treatment, as
the drugs prescribed by the second vet may be in conflict with
what the dog has already had.

House Calls

Traffic and parking problems and the time involved have
made "sending for the vet" an anachronism, at any rate in
small animal practice. There is very little the vet can do for a
dog in its home, so it is better in all ways to get the dog to the
surgery where trained staff and all the necessary equipment are
waiting. Some practices operate an animal ambulance to carry
dogs to the surgery, otherwise it will be necessary to get a taxi
if you do not have your own transport.

Veterinary surgeons will make house calls if pressed to do
so but the cost is likely to be loaded, and the dog will not be
helped very much.

If you have reason to take a dog to surgery with a condition
which may be infectious, particularly a hoarse cough which
spreads rapidly through droplets in the air, warn the surgery in
advance so that you need not go through the public waiting
room and so avoid infecting other animals.

Vomiting

Dogs vomit easily, sometimes even with pleasure. They will
eat their dinner, bring it back and eat it again — natural
behaviour which cannot be helped. They will also eat rough
grass with the intention of making themselves vomit. These
actions are quite different from compulsive sickness, when
even water is brought back. If there is also coldness, collapse
and diarrhoea, you need veterinary help fast.

Vomiting of undigested food some hours after it has been
taken also needs diagnosis quickly, but it is helpful if you can
give some idea of the pattern of the vomiting in relation to
meals, and the type of food taken.

If you know the dog has eaten some substance which may
be poisonous, take any wrapper or packet with you so that the
vet can consult the poisons unit for an antidote. If the dog has

eaten plant material, take any vomit containing residue with you as well.

A dog trying to vomit but unable to do so may be in deep trouble. Get to the veterinary surgery as quickly as you can, having warned them you are on your way.

Looseness of Bowels and Diarrhoea

Loose motions may occur from many reasons, possibly an excess of milk to drink, change of food, too much food, or too salty food causing a lot of water to be taken as well. Looseness may be caused by nerves and excitement. You can adjust all these conditions yourself; not with preparations to dry up the bowel, but by putting the puppy on to small quantities of white fish and rice (plain boiled) as a diet, and then gradually returning to small amounts of normal food until you can get a formed motion.

Diarrhoea is different; it is expelled compulsively, often explosively. There is a foul smell, usually vomiting and generalised illness as well. Keep the puppy warm, withhold food but give glucose-water to drink (1 tablespoon of glucose to 1 pint of boiled water), and get veterinary attention as soon as you can. The puppy should not walk or play, although it is unlikely to want to.

Particularly foul smelling motions containing undigested meat indicate a pancreatic deficiency, and need help at once. No punishment or reproach should ever be inflicted on a puppy with a bowel disorder; he cannot help making a mess.

Any quantity of blood in the excreta beyond a drop from a small blood vessel at the anus, should be reported to the vet very quickly.

Sore Throats and Coughs

A dog will indicate that its throat is sore by continually stretching its neck to the ceiling. If you know that it has been barking enough to make itself hoarse, or has been in sand or dusty conditions, you can treat the throat with honey licked from a spoon, and a children's cough mixture. If there are additional signs of illness, then you need the vet.

A retching sort of cough, which sounds as if a bone is stuck in the throat may mean just that — look to see. If there is no obstruction, the puppy may have kennel cough — a very infectious type of bronchial virus caught by spread of droplet from another animal — very likely to be encountered in the summer months at shows or in boarding kennels. Provided the dog is kept warm, and well fed, it will not be very ill, but the cough is tiresome and lasts for weeks. It is necessary to get antibiotic cover for a few days, and a good cough mixture.

In very young puppies kennel cough is more dangerous. Isolation will be necessary, and advice from the vet so that complications do not develop. Do not take any animal suspected of kennel cough into the surgery. Keep the dog in the car; the vet may come out to see him there rather than spread the infection to the surgery.

Cuts and Fight Wounds

Wash the blood away with correctly diluted TCP in warm water, and assess the actual damage. If your dog is constantly handled and groomed he will allow you to do anything for him. Large and deep wounds heal much quicker if they have one or two sutures (stitches), for which the dog must go to the veterinary surgery. Cover the wound with a big pad of gauze or cotton wool, and tie round with a bandage until you get the dog to the vet's. Wounds to the ear flap bleed an awful lot; you can improvise a stocking cap to keep the dog from shaking them about.

Some big dogs, notably Great Danes, will injure their tails through wagging them against walls and doors. Try to prevent this happening, as tails are very difficult to heal once opened. If a dog has a cut that he will not leave alone, or an operation wound from which he must not remove the stitches, the veterinary surgery can supply you with what is known as an Elizabethan Collar, a kind of plastic funnel which buckles round the dog's collar and encloses its head so that it cannot reach any part of its body.

Dogs seem to tolerate these collars quite well. You can take them off for short times while the dog eats or drinks. If the dog is very distressed about its collar, the vet may prescribe a tranquilliser.

Allergies

Young puppies find that they are allergic to many substances, which may vary from dyes in carpets and blankets, foods, grass and meadow plants, to reactions to the bite of a flea. It is not at all uncommon to have a puppy come in from the garden in summer with great weals of urticaria coming up rapidly all over the skin, especially in the smooth coated dogs. Although this looks dramatic, nothing need be done unless a short-nosed dog is badly affected around the nose and face, when breathing may be obstructed. You will then ask the vet to let you have some anti-histamine tablets, which are useful to have by anyway, in case a short-nosed dog gets stung in the mouth. Urticaria, or nettle rash, may be caused by many things − the most usual is falling into a bed of stinging nettles, or a dousing in cold water during hot weather. Some individuals are allergic to food substances, nearly always proteins; beef, lamb and milk have been known to give trouble. You can trace the offender by charting the foods the puppy has had which are new to it.

Rashes on the feet may be caused by allergy to pollen in grass or heather at the appropriate season, or to too strong disinfectants used in the home. Pink flushed irritation on the under-parts of the body will probably be due to something on which the puppy lies. This needs careful detective work on your part. Man-made fibres, especially acrilan carpet, may be the culprit, but it is interesting to find that it is more likely to be the mordant in the dye-stuff used than the fibre. You may find that the dog can tolerate the blue carpet, but not the red. Perhaps the offending carpet is not in your own home, but somewhere the puppy is taken to visit regularly. If you cannot trace the allergy to carpet, then look at the dog's bedding; perhaps you are using a new soap powder to wash the blankets?

Only the owner can unravel the puzzle of allergy with the veterinary surgeon, because you can give an accurate picture of the circumstances in which the dog lives. Your co-operation and active observance is all important and necessary, because if the offending substance is not found, the dog may scratch itself raw and open the way to a secondary infection which will be very difficult to clear up. It has been known that young puppies with an untraced allergy spend so much time scratching that they cannot eat, and do not grow. There is nothing externally you can do to soothe this itch which comes through the bloodstream of the dog.

Internal Pain

Pain in the stomach, intestines, or bowels is shown by a hunching up of the back, perhaps with reluctance to move, or crying out when picked up. Suspect something serious and try to take the puppy to the surgery at once, as it is likely that X-ray investigation will be needed. Do not let the puppy walk if you can avoid it.

Another sign of abdominal pain is shown when a dog assumes what is called the "praying position", bending down on the front legs, supported on the elbows, with the hind legs still upright.

Limb Pain

A limb being carried loosely, or at an awkward angle after a fall, may be fractured. It will mend very well if you get help. Reluctance to walk or a limp may mean a cyst between the toes or a thorn in the pads or a cut. Give first aid measures as you would to a human, and seek professional help next day if there is no improvement. Cysts often indicate a low state of general health, so it would be as well to have a proper examination, and possibly an antibiotic injection or vitamin B12 injection.

Muscular Pain and Joint Pain

Reluctance to walk, or small cries on getting up from sleep, may make you suspect some pain of this kind. Try to find out as much as possible about the incidence to tell the veterinary surgeon. Sometimes dogs will nibble at their legs or their back as if they had some skin trouble, but they will really be attacking the source of a pain in the joint or muscle.

Fits and Faints

Occasionally puppies will have fits, although it is less common than it was at one time. Fits may be epileptic, of hereditary origin, or may be caused by any other kind of pain, or even temper or fright. There is nothing anyone can do at the time of the fit; keep the puppy quiet, and remove him from any source of external danger, taking care not to get accidentally bitten. When the tremors have passed, you may apply ice to the head and the lips. Urine and faeces may be passed while the fit lasts. When the fit is over, leave the puppy to rest quietly and report to the veterinary surgeon over the telephone, to make an appointment for a thorough examination.

Short-faced dogs are subject to fainting fits in hot weather, or stress conditions. The dog may well fall down on its side in mid-gallop, or while greeting its master. Keep calm, and apply the ice treatment, all round the head and the back of the neck. The dog will recover very soon, but I would want the vet to check its heart action, to see there are no physical defects. A puppy that faints often, or that must rest frequently when out at exercise, or fails to grow properly while eating well, needs investigation for malfunction of the heart.

13.

Feeding a Puppy

The majority of dogs today are fed either on ready-prepared canned food or on commercially formulated dry diets. These foods take all the guesswork out of preparing home cooked diets involving weighing and working out of percentages and component elements together with additional vitamins and minerals.

The top brands of commercially formulated diets contain all the elements a dog needs. Most of the manufacturers present different formulations for puppies, growing dogs, breeding bitches, geriatric dogs and those which need to lose weight. For the owner, the benefit is the removal of the need to buy and store fresh meat and other ingredients and the guesswork of adding vitamins and minerals. Too generous a helping of these additives can cause the dog serious harm, so most owners are very glad to have the nutritionally complete formulas prepared for them. Clean to handle and store, the dry diets save on shopping time and refrigerator space and take away the need to keep animal-quality meat away from foods destined for human consumption.

Your puppy may well have been reared on one of these

complete diets. You will find that they are highly digestible, and low in bulk, and there is far less waste material expelled in faeces. Your veterinary surgery may well be selling the top grade complete diets.

A dog can live and thrive on these diets for the whole of its life, but in order to prevent boredom, some owners will like to add small quantities of household scraps such as cheese, meat trimmings, white fish, cooked eggs or chicken stock. Do not give milk; most adult dogs cannot digest milk and giving milk is often the cause of loose motions.

Where dogs suffer from food allergies, it is nearly always beef, wheat, soya bean or dairy products which cause the allergy. For these dogs it is possible to obtain a complete diet which contains only lamb meat and rice − a great saving in human time and energy and also an excellent meal for the dog.

Complete diets are fed in unbelievably small quantities because they are so energy-dense. A Labrador weighing 40 lbs will need only about 8 oz of a good complete diet each day, together with ample access to water. Do not forget these diets are *dry;* you are not buying water in them, but the dog will require plenty of water to drink.

It is preferable never to give a dog real meat bones. Bones make for quarrels, between animals and between dogs and humans. In fact they bring out the worst in a dog's character and it is better not to make this trigger to possessive behaviour available. Besides that, bones smell and may become fly-blown, so it is better not to have them around. A good hard nylon bone is just as good for the teeth.

14.

Introducing Puppy to Other Pets

Will your cat take offence if you introduce a new puppy into your home? The answer has to be, almost certainly he will, but if you are fortunate, the hostility will be only temporary. Puppies are inquisitive and may try to be too friendly too soon with your cat. The puppy is likely to get spat at and be batted with a paw for his pains but serious injury is unlikely as puppies are usually bundles of thick fur which protects them to a large extent, and it is surprising how rarely there are scratches which land on the puppy's eyes. Your best ploy is to create a very comfortable bed for the cat high up, well out of the puppy's way. Cats like to sit on top of a high refrigerator or cupboard, so make the new bed as inviting as you can and it is likely that the cat will watch the puppy's antics from on high and will, in its own good time, come down to floor level to fraternise. Cats and puppies can end up as very good friends, sharing a bed and being a comfort to each other.

Always feed the cat separately, preferably in its high level accommodation, and do not leave cat food down all day or the puppy will surely eat it all, in addition to its own carefully worked out food allowance. Make sure the cat's indoor litter tray is not accessible to the puppy; cat faeces are very attractive to other animals and you do not want the puppy to acquire a repulsive habit of this kind if you can avoid it.

If your cat is really deeply offended at the addition to the family it may decide to leave home and apply to a nearby house to be taken in and fed. If this happens, make enquiries round the neighbourhood; it is likely that your cat is living in someone's house nearby.

The other weapon which a male cat has in its armoury is to take to "spraying" an especially highly pungent type of urine indoors. This is territory marking to establish what it hopes is sole ownership of the home. Consult your veterinary surgeon about this anti-social behaviour as a lot more is understood now about feline behaviour patterns and it may be that either the vet, or a specialist in cat behaviour to whom you can be referred will be able to help you arrive at a happy solution.

Puppy and Older Dog

There are lots of reasons for getting a puppy as company for a dog already established in your home. If you are truly devoted to dogs you may realise that the life of a dog is very short compared with our own, ten to twelve years being a good average age. You may also feel that the desolation of being without a dog at all is very hard to bear, so when your old favourite is getting old, it is a very good idea to acquire a new puppy to continue the family tradition. When the older dog is about eight years old is a sensible stage to consider getting a puppy. You will find that the older dog will renew its youth to some extent, stimulated by having a young member of its own species around the house, and the older dog can definitely help in training the young one, in house training, come-when-called, lead walking and staying quietly when you are out. A bitch will be especially good with a puppy. Her maternal feelings will surface even if she has never had a litter of her own. It is a good idea to take your older dog with you to collect the puppy, so that they can meet on neutral ground and the older dog can bring the puppy into his or her territory. Make up two beds, but it will be only a short time before you find them curled up together, and the puppy being washed by its foster mother or father. Again, make sure you feed the two separately and do not let the puppy raid the adult's dish, as that may bring out hostile feelings which would otherwise never surface. Do give the older dog "time off" from being tormented by the puppy, when it becomes more active. Make sure you take the older dog out with you, or allow it time with you in another room... even nannies want some time off!

Nearly all dogs accept a young puppy very happily, but if your adult dog is a male, problems may well arise when the puppy is becoming adolescent. There can be rivalry and bids for dominance by the younger dog. This situation can escalate into ugly fights, not constantly, but breaking out at highly inconvenient times, such as when visitors have just arrived at the house and tensions are high. Rivalry between male dogs is most common in the guarding and territorially dominant breeds, and it occurs more rarely in gundogs or hounds which retain their hereditary pack behaviour to a greater degree. Toy dogs are not so prone to fight either, and the genial Cavalier King Charles Spaniel is the easiest of all when it comes to males living happily together in the same home.

Puppy and horse

Introductions to horses and goats should be managed slowly and carefully, with the owner always present and watchful. Horses are very interested in puppies, but all these species should preferably meet with a stable half-door or a sound fence between the two so they may sniff and exchange pleasantries without the need to be defensive. Never let a dog chase horses or run loose among them; a sharp kick can so easily break a dog's leg. It is very useful to take your dog, securely held on a lead, to an agricultural show or livestock sale, so that while under strict control your young dog can get used to the sounds and smells of other creatures.

15.

Introducing Puppy to Baby

Many women feel that to have a puppy during their pregnancy is ideal and so it can be, but there are some special considerations to have in mind. One is not to cultivate an especially strong bond between you and the puppy when you know that your time and your affection will have to be shared in the future. It is a wise precaution to share the puppy care with friends and other members of the family. Let a friend take the puppy out sometimes, make sure the puppy becomes as attached to your partner as it does to you. A dog behaviour counsellor who has made a speciality of dog and baby problems advises that you cuddle a teddy bear and talk to it lovingly so that your puppy is aware it cannot monopolise your attention.

When educating your puppy in social manners it is important to teach the little dog not to jump up, not to snatch food, and not to lie across doorways where you may stumble over him. Talk to the puppy a lot but do not excite him or allow other people to do so. Rough games are definitely not to be encouraged, but throwing a toy which the dog will bring back can give a lot of exercise to the pup while you are sitting down.

Likewise a version of "hunt the slipper" (or the biscuit) provides exercise for body and brain. In view of the impending new arrival of the baby, it is best if squeaky toys are not given to the puppy, so there is no confusion in the dog's mind. If during pregnancy you are able to spend a lot of time teaching the puppy different behaviour patterns, with emphasis on sit, lie down and GET IN YOUR BED, both you and your dog will achieve a lot during the waiting time.

It is unfortunate and very sad that one of the more common reasons for getting rid of a well-loved dog is due to pressure by older relatives when they hear a young woman is pregnant. Quite often the mother-to-be wants to keep her canine friend but is made to feel that she puts her baby at risk by doing so. It just is not true! A dog is very much part of the family ambiance and many grown people today recall with pleasure the dog of their childhood, to the extent of buying a puppy "just like old Kim" when they are grown up themselves. Well kept family dogs are not sources of infection, nor are they biting machines if they are properly educated, and to bring up a baby to fear dogs is to give it an automatic handicap for later life. So do resist the well-meant advice to dispose of the dog once pregnancy is confirmed.

An indoor folding kennel, more familiarly known as a crate, is invaluable for a puppy anyway, but doubly so when you may need to know your young dog is safely confined when you are busy elsewhere. Dogs simply love their crates; they represent the safety and sanctity of the den of a free living animal. One of the great advantages is that the crate can be quickly dismantled and taken to any room in the house, so the dog need not be shut away from where the action is; it can be where it can see and be seen, and where it can be talked to, no matter what is going on. Make the crate comfortable with a bean bag or rug, and in winter stand it against a radiator. Feed the dog in the crate, put titbits and toys there, so the dog learns to make its headquarters within the house. To begin with leave the door open, but then when the dog is comfortable with using the crate, shut the door occasionally for a short time, which you

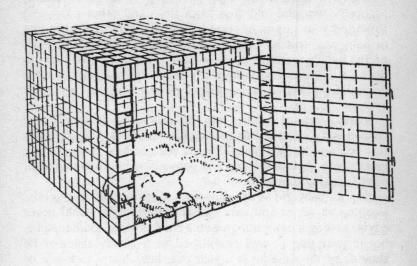

Figure 3.   Indoor kennels

Wire cages for enclosing the pup for short periods. They soon become a favourite 'home' and can be collapsed into a flat package for storage or removal.

can extend at will as necessary, but never to the limits of confining the dog for hours at a time. Dogs never soil their beds, so prolonged incarceration in a relatively small space is a cruelty.

When the baby arrives, involve your dog in your care of the baby as much as possible. Let him be with you while you feed and attend to the baby, the dog in his crate or, if necessary, tied to a chair if he has not learnt "sit" quite perfectly enough. Looking at the new situation from the dog's point of view, there is a completely new scent, and many new sounds in the house, new vehicles on wheels indoors, and something new taking your attention. Let the dog smell the baby, let it watch the baby-care. Talk to the dog while you are busy. Hold a calm, unexciting conversation.

You will have made sure your dog is in good health, regularly wormed and free from fleas and other parasites. Provided your dog is in good health, there is very little dog or baby can "catch" from each other, and a few gentle licks on the baby's arm will do it no harm. You may even want to throw a titbit or two, ostensibly from the baby, so that the dog thinks this new arrival is a good thing from his own point of view.

Always reward quiet, calm behaviour with kindly eye contact and a smile so that the dog knows he has your approval, that you and he still have a happy partnership. Even so, you must never, *never* leave dog and baby alone in the same room. That is taking tolerance too far.

As your baby grows up, allow him to stroke your dog gently, teaching as far as you can, gentle behaviour. I would never advise getting a new puppy when a child is at the toddler stage, but if your dog is well-established as a family member he should, by the time he is a year old, have learnt to evade or endure the worst the baby can inflict upon him!

Toddlers are exploring their own world, learning their own skills, and they have a long way to go before they learn to do what they are told, or not to do, as the case may be. They have no idea at all about cruelty, but many, many of the unhappy incidents involving dogs and children are in fact brought about by the child inflicting cruelty upon the dog. Dogs can be exceedingly patient with young children, but unsupervised play should never be allowed. A toddler will find it hard to differentiate between a large stuffed toy and a living dog... but a dog can be badly hurt by having a child bounce on its back, or bend its legs at awkward angles. Sharp sticks poked into eyes or ears, rubber bands embedded in the fur of the neck or the legs, all cause excruciating agony and sometimes induce the dog to take defensive action. The dog will pay with its life if it even marks the skin of a child, but quite often the dog has been tormented to the limit of its endurance.

Once more, it is important to pay extra attention to the dog's health and to ask the vet to give check-ups regularly. Painful gums and teeth, or sore inflamed ears can cause a dog to react badly to being touched roughly on a sensitive place.

Other Children

When your child reaches the stage of having other children in to play, it is a wise precaution to keep the dog in a separate room. Games in the garden can become wildly exciting, and unfamiliar and shrill voices add to the tension. A child can be easily knocked down and hurt although the dog did not mean any harm.

The guarding breeds in particular may object to other children playing with the family toys. Your dog will guard his children and their possessions and this too can lead to misunderstandings which lead to physical harm. Always take the precautions which save your dog and save your child from getting into trouble. Many disasters stem from the unconscious desire to demonstrate that your dog and your child are perfectly behaved. Both can behave unwisely, both can make unwitting errors of judgement which lead them and you into trouble of the worst kind.

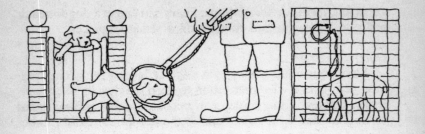

16.

Rescued Dogs

Taking on a rescued or homeless dog is a good deed but like all worthwhile good deeds, it is not easy.

All dogs require a lot of patience on the part of their owners, but your rescued, or secondhand, dog may well need more than the average amount of sympathy and tolerance.

You may find mongrel puppies as young as eight weeks old available for re-homing in some rescue shelters. They may have been hand reared by the staff after being found abandoned, or they may have been handed in for re-homing by someone whose bitch was accidentally mated. It is likely that these puppies will be well socialised by the staff, but you are unlikely to have the advantage of seeing the sire or the dam to assess their temperament, and it is probable that these puppies will not have had the opportunity to adapt to all the sounds of a household. It is not unusual to find that puppies which have been kennel reared are terrified of the noise of a vacuum cleaner or a washing machine.

A puppy like this will need abundant sympathy and understanding. In this context sympathy does not mean an excess of cuddles, it means understanding the limits of communication between you and your dog, and a great deal of tolerance in appreciating the difficulty your dog has in learning to live in a completely new environment. Rather than sympathising with the dog, you should jolly it along, talk brightly to it, offer a biscuit, convey in every way you can that life alongside noisy household appliances is good.

You will, of course, take every precaution that your rescued puppy cannot escape, because unfamiliar noises can cause a highly strung dog to panic and achieve spectacular feats in terms of jumping fences and running away. The puppy's dam may have been of an exceedingly nervous disposition, or she may have been harshly treated, may even have been "living rough" when the puppies were born. Her puppies will have inherited some of their dam's fears and prejudices. I took on a rescued dog once who was only happy when sitting in a car, because, I found later, an old broken-down car had been home to the bitch and puppies. When kept in a house, she was panicked and barked the whole time and it took a long while to break down her prejudices.

It will be rare to find an eight week old pedigree puppy in a rescue home, although possibly one which is not acceptable to the Kennel Club standard, for instance a white Boxer or a parti-coloured Poodle, may be unwanted. Nearly all the clubs catering for pedigree breeds run their own rescue services, organised, managed, funded and worked entirely by volunteers. The Kennel Club will give you a list of Breed Club Rescue organisations and their officials, but be warned, the investigations you will have to survive are much more intensive than when you buy a puppy direct from a breeder. In most cases a breed club member will come to visit you, to check on your lifestyle and your house and garden from a safety point of view. They may well bring a dog of their own with them, with the object of showing you what an adult member of your favoured breed would be like in your personal surroundings. This can be quite important, as some aspect of size or coat length and texture may not appeal to you after all, and it is better to be forewarned than to realise afterwards that you have made a mistake and that you are not happy with the dog.

Do not feel embarrassed or indignant about being asked searching questions about your family, your home and your lifestyle when you are being interviewed about your suitability to take on a rescued dog. Breed rescuers have been entrusted to find second or even third homes for dogs which have had a bad start in life, probably through no fault of their own. It is all too easy to be emotionally touched by the sight of unwanted dogs eagerly waiting in case you have come for them, or to feel great sympathy for a dog from your favourite breed which is disadvantaged in some way. It is very easy to lose touch with reality in such a situation, to fail to appreciate just what taking on such a dog can mean.

When talking to you and your partner frankly while visiting your home, asking questions which you may resent, the adoption counsellor has the dog's welfare in mind, and also your own welfare, because making a mistake could be costly to you in terms of house destruction and annoyance to neighbours and visitors. There are many people who would love to have a dog to come home to at night and to take walking at weekends, and no doubt the dog would have a super home at those times. But thousands of people do not have time in their busy lives to give enough time to a dog, especially to a rescued dog which has known other owners. The rescued dog's most important need is for security and the constant companionship of caring owners. The most common reasons for dogs needing re-homing are:

1. Breakup of partnerships and re-location of homes and employment making dog ownership impossible.
2. An unwise buy, destructive behaviour while unsupervised and lonely. Constant barking, annoying neighbours.
3. Aggression towards people, often a particular category of people, possibly men, children, ethnic minorities, people in uniforms, people carrying large parcels, etc.
4. Persistent house training problems because not enough time was spent teaching the dog as a young puppy.

5. Aggression towards other dogs to the extent that the dog cannot be exercised in public places.
6. Livestock chasing, unsafe with sheep, poultry, cats.

These failings are not always frankly revealed when seeking to re-home a dog. It is obvious that none of these bad habits and learned bad behaviour patterns can be unlearnt unless someone perceptive, observant and kind is available to keep the dog company for most of the day. Dogs never reform their characters on their own. They only get worse unless there is someone around to tell them NO!

What a dog needs most from you is your *time*. If you do not have time to spend on him, and with him, winter and summer, weekdays as well as weekends, then be firm with yourself and leave the dog where he is. There is nothing more sad than having to return a second-chance dog to wait for yet another offer of a home. Each experience in a different home with different geography and a different set of rules diminishes the dog's chance of ever having a stable relationship with the right family.

Pedigree breed rescue organisations rarely have kennels where you can see the dogs on offer. Frequently owners who wish to dispose of their dogs are persuaded to keep them until they can be placed with new owners. This is the least distressing procedure for the dog and for the new owners, because the dog will not have the distress of going into kennels and possibly losing house training and acquiring barking habits it may not have had before.

Many pedigree breed rescues also have foster homes with people who have an understanding of a particular breed, and so can assess the dog for temperament and health. If you apply for a dog you will be told what is available and what will suit you; rarely are you able to have any choice except acceptance or refusal. At a large dog home where the majority of dogs and puppies looking for homes will be mongrel, it is usually possible to walk around and choose the dog which appeals to you most but even so, you will have to answer a lot of questions and probably receive a home visit before you are judged to be suitable to take a dog.

It is possible to make contact with owners who want to part with their dogs through the local press, and this may be the most satisfactory way of acquiring a dog but in that case, it is you who will have to carry out the in-depth questioning about reasons and motives for no longer wanting the dog. "Emigrating" is the favourite excuse, but will they actually go away permanently? You have to make your own judgements and you may want to stipulate that you will take the dog on trial to see if he settles with you. Pedigree dog rescue organisations very rarely give the pedigree papers with dogs they re-home and some, on principle, retain nominal ownership of the dog and stipulate that it must come back to them if ever you cannot cope. If the rescue organisation can possibly afford it, the aim is to have all bitches spayed before they leave the rescue home, to prevent exploitation by breeding, but dogs are rarely castrated.

Rescued dogs are not free to new homes, but even a pedigree puppy loses value quite quickly after it is past the baby puppy stage so no-one parting with a pedigree puppy can expect anything like their money back, and certainly not any recompense for the money expended upon it so far. Substantial donations to the rescue funds are quite rightly expected, and possibly some evidence that you can afford to keep the dog.

The kennel staff or the rescue helpers will tell you all they know about the dog, from the previous history they were given and from their observations of the dog while it has been in kennels. But this information can only be a guide line. The dog you have chosen may have a number of secrets which you will only discover after many weeks of living together. You will want to observe your new dog carefully, to watch his reactions to all kinds of ordinary as well as emergency happenings within your home or outside. From watching and under-standing you will eventually build up a picture of your dog's past history, his fears and his enthusiasms, his strengths and weaknesses.

Take great care of your new dog on the journey to your home and in the first few days with you. Pedigree dogs are usually delivered direct to the new home by a member of the rescue chain. This gives them the opportunity to satisfy themselves that the dog will settle with you.

Dogs, particularly those of the hound breeds, may have enjoyed living free where there was a plentiful source of wild food and some shelter. Unless the dog has been injured by a car or met with some other disaster, free running is back to nature for some types of dog and it may not appreciate the fact that it is now confined. You may find your new acquisition is eager to escape again, so take all precautions.

Put a strong well-fitting collar and lead, complete with identity disc with your address, on to the dog before you leave the kennels and resolve that you will not let the dog off the lead in a park or in the country for several weeks. Until you know how your new dog will react to everyday challenges, like traffic noise, passing horses, motorbikes, cyclists wearing helmets, joggers, prams and children, as well as other dogs, you must have lead control as well as being on the alert to take evasive action so that your dog does not get itself, or you, into trouble. Train the family to shut the dog in a safe room before they open the front door... always! This applies to a newly bought puppy too; they can dash out before you are even aware they are there.

Teach the children not to bend down to the dog, not to take any chances with him until he has settled in, not to disturb him while he is eating, and not to remove the feeding bowl until the dog has left it and moved away. Be careful not to startle the dog with loud noises, not to scream or shout, nor excite the dog with rough play. Be careful when picking up garden tools, brooms and sticks, your new dog may have bad memories of chastisement with similar things.

Work out what your dog language will be and be consistent in using the words you decide upon. Do not attempt to start formal obedience training at this time; wait until you and the dog are an established partnership before you put any strains on the relationship.

If only your new pet could sit down and tell you what his life history has been, taking him into your family would be so much easier, but you have to find out the hard way, by trial and some error. Do not take any liberties with the dog at first, and reduce the stress your new pet is bound to feel as much as you can. Keep the atmosphere cool, do not rush at the dog with affection. Let him find out about his new environment and you start finding out about him. A dog which has become homeless through a partnership break-up may become extremely worried at raised voices, quarrels and tears. Take warning from grumbles and growling, and baring of teeth. This is no time to give punishment. Just watch what caused the reaction and make up your mind whether this can be trained out or whether your dog has a behaviour pattern which will be dangerous to live with.

Preventing mistakes is the keynote. Give your new dog every chance to be right, and to make good in his new home. Remember that ingrained and often undesirable behaviour patterns may still show up for the first time when your dog has been with you for many weeks. When he feels secure, he may try to test your tolerance. Do not relax your vigilance on him until you are quite confident that you know the dog really well. Above all, do not leave the dog with playing children at any time. Never take any risks. Eventually you will have the satisfaction of having given a dog the second chance he deserved to make good.

17.

Dog Shows

Every weekend and sometimes in mid-week there are dog shows, in various grades, all round the country. Many people enjoy the competitive element and make dog showing not only their leisure activity but find their social life in this scene too. In fact, you can be a very important person in the dog show world even if you do not have a dog, as an official of the organisation or as a steward to the judges, but obviously it is much more fun if you can enter the competitions.

With the exception of the lowest level of shows, every dog entered must be registered at the Kennel Club. Dogs are eligible to compete in the Puppy class when they are six months old and from then on, they are entered in graded classes according to age or the amount they have won.

Dog showing is not a cheap hobby and the prize money, if any, is negligible. Entries have to be made as much as two months ahead, so it is quite possible that the entry will be wasted if you or your dog are not on top form on the day. The real benefit of dog showing is pride in having a dog which can beat ten or twenty (or even more) others. A top winning dog will be in demand at stud, and his worth will increase dramatically should you wish to sell him overseas, but not many owners want to do so. The progeny of a consistently winning top dog command higher prices, and the owner will probably be offered many judging appointments, even some expenses-paid overseas trips, so that is where the reward comes in. But it is not easy to keep at this level unless you have a kennel of dogs to select from, so if the dog you bought as a pet should prove to be a show winner, enjoy it while you can!

Both owner and dog must have a talent for showing themselves off at their best. Some dogs love showing, others make it very clear they would rather stay at home. It is very rewarding if the owner or a near relative should prove to be what is known as "a good handler", skilled at hiding the dog's faults from the judge's eye, and presenting the dog with flair and flourish. But unlike the dog, which must rest upon its own attributes, it is possible for the owner to engage a professional handler who will train the dog to show and then take it into the show ring on the owner's behalf.

It is not easy to buy a show-worthy puppy for your first dog. You may ask the breeder for a puppy suitable to show, but very often the good looking puppy does not fulfill its early promise. However, by the time you are ready to buy another pup you will know more what you should be looking for, and from a study of pedigrees and winners you will be familiar with the type and the lines that you want.

You learn to handle your puppy at what is known as a "ringcraft class", run by your local dog club. As well as general training for showing, and instruction on how and where to enter (and how to play the strategy game about which judges may favour your dog's type), you will also enter friendly matches, just one dog against another, which give you a taste of the competitive side, and also help to train novice judges. Suggestions may be made as to where you can make your first entry in a public show, or possibly at a show confined to your own breed. Once you have been awarded one of those coveted rosettes, you will be eagerly anticipating another weekend, another show. Details of shows to come and the judges officiating will be found in Dog World and Our Dogs, the weekly newspapers of the fancy.

Even if your dog does not turn out to be a beauty, you can still have lots of fun in agility competitions which are open to both pedigree dogs and mongrels. The owner or handler runs round, encouraging the dog, while it goes over jumps, crawls through tunnels, balances on a see-saw and negotiates other obstacles, aiming to beat the minimum time taken by the other entrants as well as avoiding knocking any obstacle down. It is great fun and the dogs love it, and once more you can bask in the pride of being part of a winning team. Your local canine society or a veterinary surgery can tell you where the nearest agility club is held.

Maybe you will not want to compete in public, but when your dog is fully grown you can make up a mini agility course in your garden, which will provide useful exercise for both the dog and the children. Puppies under a year old should not be asked to negotiate agility obstacles, as putting too much stress on growing joints and muscles is not wise.

Your dog will take up quite a lot of your time; he will also be a very big interest and feature in the life of the whole family. Perhaps he will add a complete new dimension to your pleasure in taking exercise, and in meeting new friends who are attracted to you through the dog. I hope that the puppy you have bought so carefully and trained so patiently will be your pride and joy for many years, for you will have joined the ranks of the millions of people throughout the world who 'have given their hearts to a dog to tear'.

Useful Addresses

The Kennel Club, 1 Clarges Street, London W1
Tel: 0171 493 6651
For registration or transfer of ownership of your puppy; will
also provide a list of breeders, and of breed clubs which may
be interesting for you to join. Most provide a newsletter once
or twice a year, talks on the breed and parties for dogs and
owners.

Pet Plan Puppyline, 10/13 Heathfield Terrace, Chiswick,
London W4 4JE   Tel: 0181 742 7442
Puppyline will post to you on request a list of breeders with
puppies for sale which is updated daily. A small charge is made
to cover administration.

The National Dog Register, c/o Wood Green Animal Shelters,
London Road, Godmanchester, Huntingdon, Cambridgeshire
Tel: 01480 830566
Keeps the particulars of owners of dogs which have been
identichipped.

National Dog Tattoo Register, Trenarren, Mersea Road,
Langenhoe, Colchester, C05 7LL   Tel: 01206 735336

Royal Society For Prevention of Cruelty to Animals, The
Manor House, The Causeway, Horsham, Sussex, RH12 1HG
Tel: 01403 264181

National Canine Defence League, 1 & 2 Pratt Mews,
London, NW1 0AD   Tel: 0171 388 0137

Engraved Dog Tags (see National Canine Defence League)

Animal Aunts, c/o Gillie McNichol, Wydwooch, 45 Fairview Road, Headley Down, Hampshire, GU35 8HQ.
Tel: 01428 712611
Will come and look after your house and pets when you have to be away.

Complete Dog Foods: Eukanuba
Leander International Kennels   Tel: 01273 833390
Hills Pet Products (Science Dept)   Tel: 0800 282 438

Dog Newspapers
Our Dogs and *Dog World* are published weekly. They contain news of dog shows and advertisements for all dog needs and equipment.
Dogs Today and *Dogs Monthly* are glossy magazines to be found on bookstalls. They carry a lot of material and advertisements of interest to pet owners.

Breeders' Kennel Stationery, 9 Imber Road, Bratton, nr Westbury, Wiltshire, BA13 4SH   Tel: 01380 831221
Writing paper, pedigree forms, etc, with breed insignia to make it really personal.

Index

In our Paperfronts series
(standard paperback size)

HOW TO HAVE A
WELL-MANNERED DOG

Kay White & J M Evans, M.R.C.V.S.

The ill-mannered dog is a curse. Fouling pavements, knocking children off their bicycles, jumping up at visitors, barking for hours on end, chewing the woodwork — all these and many other unattractive habits bring the canine race into disrepute.

As Kay White and Jim Evans explain in this book, all this can be avoided by *proper management,* from the first day the puppy comes home. Get the puppy to understand that *you* are the pack leader. Understand how the puppy *thinks.*

Even if the dog is a little older, all is not lost. Specially written sections on preventing bad habits and curing problem behaviour will greatly benefit the more mature dog, and his owner!

Co-written by author of Choose & Bring Up Your Puppy

RIGHT WAY
PUBLISHING POLICY

HOW WE SELECT TITLES

RIGHT WAY consider carefully every deserving manuscript. Where an author is an authority on his subject but an inexperienced writer, we provide first-class editorial help. The standards we set make sure that every **RIGHT WAY** book is practical, easy to understand, concise, informative and delightful to read. Our specialist artists are skilled at creating simple illustrations which augment the text wherever necessary.

CONSISTENT QUALITY

At every reprint our books are updated where appropriate, giving our authors the opportunity to include new information.

FAST DELIVERY

We sell **RIGHT WAY** books to the best bookshops throughout the world. It may be that your bookseller has run out of stock of a particular title. If so, he can order more from us at any time — we have a fine reputation for "same day" despatch, and we supply any order, however small (even a single copy), to any bookseller who has an account with us. We prefer you to buy from your bookseller, as this reminds him of the strong underlying public demand for **RIGHT WAY** books. Readers who live in remote places, or who are housebound, or whose local bookseller is unco-operative, can order direct from us by post.

FREE

If you would like an up-to-date list of all **RIGHT WAY** titles currently available, send a stamped self-addressed envelope to

ELLIOT RIGHT WAY BOOKS,
KINGSWOOD, SURREY, KT20 6TD, U.K.